Best American Short Plays Series

THE
BEST
AMERICAN
SHORT
PLAYS
1999–2000

edited by
GLENN YOUNG

An Applause Original

THE BEST AMERICAN SHORT PLAYS 1999-2000

No part of this publication may be reproduced or transmitted in any form or by any means, electronic or mechanical, including photocopy, recording, or any information storage or retrieval system now known to be invented, without permission in writing from the publishers, except by a reviewer who wishes to quote brief passages in connection with a review written for inclusion in a magazine, newspaper or broadcast.

NOTE: All plays contained in this volume are fully protected under the Copyright Laws of the United States of America, the British Empire, including the Dominion of Canada, and all other countries of the International Copyright Union and the Universal Copyright Convention. Permission to reproduce, wholly or in part, by any method, must be obtained from the copyright owners or their agents. (See CAUTION notices at the beginning of each play.)

Copyright ©2001 by Applause Theatre Book Publishers
All Rights Reserved
ISBN 1-55783-451-2 (cloth), 1-55783-452-0 (paper)
ISSN 0067-6284

**APPLAUSE THEATRE &
CINEMA BOOKS**
151 W46th Street, 8th Floor
New York, NY 10036
Phone: (212) 575-9265
FAX: (646) 562-5852
email: info@applausepub.com

COMBINED BOOK SERVICES
LTD.
Units I/K, Paddock Wood
Distribution Centre
Paddock Wood, Tonbridge,
Kent TN 12 6UU
Phone: (44) 01892 837171
Fax: (44) 01892 837272

SALES & DISTRIBUTION, HAL LEONARD CORP.
7777 West Bluemound Road, P.O. Box 13819
Milwaukee, WI 53213
Phone: (414) 774-3630 Fax: (414) 774-3259
email:halinfo@halleonard.com
internet: www.halleonard.com

Best American Short Plays Series

THE
BEST
AMERICAN
SHORT
PLAYS
1999–2000

edited by

GLENN YOUNG

APPLAUSE

NEW YORK • LONDON

CONTENTS

Billy Aronson

LIGHT YEARS

Billy Aronson

Billy Aronson's plays have been published in *Best American Short Plays 92-93*, *Plays From Woolly Mammoth Theatre*, and *Ensemble Studio Theatre Marathon 2000*, and awarded a NYFA grant. His writing for the musical theater includes the original concept and additional lyrics for the Broadway musical *Rent*, and librettos for operas commissioned by American Opera Projects with music by Rusty Magee and Kitty Brazelton. His TV writing includes scripts for CTW, MTV, and the Cartoon Network. Playwrights Horizons, Inc., New York City, produced the World Premiere of *Light Years* Off-Broadway in 2001. A member of Ensemble Studio Theater and the Dramatists Guild, Billy lives in Brooklyn with his wife Lisa Vogel and their children Jake and Anna.

"*Light Years*" is the first act of a full-length play also called *Light Years*.

The one-act "*Light Years*" was originally presented by Ensemble Studio Theatre, Curt Dempster Artistic Director and Jamie Richards Executive Producer. The production featured Sarah Rose, Anne Marie Nest, Paul Bartholomew, and Ian Reed Kesler, under the direction of Jamie Richards.

CHARACTERS

Four college students:
COURTNEY
DAPHNE
DOUG
MICHAEL

TIME: *Beginning of freshman year, about 6 P.M.*

SETTING: *Living room of a freshman double. Door to bedroom. Door to hall. Desk with chair. Closet. Couch. Crate.* DAPHNE & COURTNEY.

DAPHNE: So if I wear these sunglasses —

COURTNEY: Philosophy.

DAPHNE: They'll see me as —

COURTNEY: Lit major, comp lit, philosophy, psych.

DAPHNE: But if I go with this pair —

COURTNEY: Engineer.

DAPHNE: Engineer.

COURTNEY: Exactly.

DAPHNE: So I have …

COURTNEY: The choice.

DAPHNE: Right.

COURTNEY: Deep or diligent.

DAPHNE: [*Thinks.*]

COURTNEY: Or you could go to the picnic open, like me. Open to sunshine. Open to the breeze. Open to law school.

DAPHNE: Right.

COURTNEY: Any choice has its pluses. I'm just saying that before you get pegged, you should decide.

DAPHNE: Right.

COURTNEY: Same goes for the photo.

DAPHNE: The photo.

COURTNEY: On your desk.

DAPHNE: Oh yeah.

COURTNEY: That photo says, to those dropping by on their way to the picnic, that you have someone, and that you're taken.

DAPHNE: Right.

COURTNEY: I have lots of someones. But I'm not taken.

DAPHNE: Right.

COURTNEY: I have friends who are taken, but want to appear untaken. That's their business.

DAPHNE: Right.

COURTNEY: I even have a friend who has no one, but wants to appear taken, for strategic purposes.

DAPHNE: Right.

COURTNEY: So anything goes. It's all up to you.

DAPHNE: [*Nods.*]

COURTNEY: So? Do you want to appear taken?

DAPHNE: [*Thinks.*]

COURTNEY: Let's work backwards. Do you have someone?

DAPHNE: [*Thinks.*]

COURTNEY: Have you ever had someone?

DAPHNE: This guy, we'd talk about everything, one time it was raining and there were all these sounds, the noises were us, saying and doing those things, that people say and do.

COURTNEY: So you have had someone.

DAPHNE: I can't remember.

COURTNEY: But you do want to have someone.

DAPHNE: Yes. Yes.

COURTNEY: So you'll put away the photo.

DAPHNE: Right.

COURTNEY: And the cross.

DAPHNE: The ...

COURTNEY: Around your neck.

DAPHNE: This is a cross?

COURTNEY: It looks like a cross.

DAPHNE: Right.

COURTNEY: I'm not saying bury it, I'm just saying be aware.

DAPHNE: Aware.

COURTNEY: Of the whole question.

DAPHNE: Uh huh ...

COURTNEY: Born again. Or the other extreme. Free spirit.

DAPHNE: Right.

COURTNEY: We're talking about your most fundamental values.

DAPHNE: My most fundamental values.

COURTNEY: Exactly.

DAPHNE: Which are ...

COURTNEY: Pursuit of truth. Love of humanity. I don't know.

DAPHNE: Right.

COURTNEY: Before heading to the picnic you need to ask yourself: is that symbol rooted in the exact message you want to send out?

DAPHNE: Right.

COURTNEY: So?

DAPHNE: I'll come up with the answers as we shop for a plant.

COURTNEY: Shop for a plant? Now?

DAPHNE: [*Sits frozen.*]

COURTNEY: Are you telling me … you want to skip the freshmen picnic?

DAPHNE: [*Sits frozen.*]

COURTNEY: Daphne. Outside that window, in a matter of minutes, our generation will assemble. For this chance to win a prime spot in their ranks you've spent your last three summers serving burgers, committed your Fridays to filing periodicals, and taken out loans you'll be repaying til you're disabled or forty or dead. So seize the moment. Select the impression that will leap from your front and ricochet through the crowd til you're burned in their brains as a —

DAPHNE: Philosophical lit major who's not religious and not taken.

COURTNEY: Good. So then …

DAPHNE: I can't put away the photo. Because I can't stand up. My legs, something funny. I can crawl, I'm crawling.

COURTNEY: Listen to me. Daphne. You'll be fine, because you're blessed with something that will get you through no matter what the world throws at you: You're pure.

DAPHNE: Pure what.

COURTNEY: Inside you, is a basic goodness and honesty that's special.

DAPHNE: You see this after knowing me for two hours?

COURTNEY: I saw this after knowing you for two seconds. The things I'm encouraging you to consider are icing on the cake. That's all. We just want the right icing, for so very fine a cake.

DAPHNE: [*Sitting up.*] This is all so easy for you.

COURTNEY: You think I'm the type who just, everything's easy?

DAPHNE: I didn't mean anything bad.

COURTNEY: I know you didn't. It's only that some people have tended to label me. You know. As the type. Gliding along. Not really meaning things. But the thing is, growing up, my mother couldn't be with us so I, always had to be the one smiling, but it isn't easy always being the one smiling, people don't realize that, but I need you to know that when I say things to you I really mean those things from my heart.

DAPHNE: I know that.

COURTNEY: Anyway. Before I open the door to let in potential escorts, let's both take a second.

[*They sit. A "Special Song" plays from above. Instantly, both go into a trance.*]

COURTNEY: Somebody upstairs has good taste in songs.

[*They listen.*]

DAPHNE: Sleeping late on a snow day.

COURTNEY: Driving home from the prom.

[*When the song fades, they emerge from their trances.* COURTNEY *opens the door — to find* DOUG *standing there.* DOUG *raises his voice at the end of many declarative sentences so they sound like questions.*]

DOUG: The sunshine splashing across the banners? The flowers all over the place?, and everywhere you look the greatest people? Strumming guitars? Dancing around? Hugging? Every few steps a different song? Everyone so giving, so open? Can I come in?, great room, so near the main entrance?, so near the bathroom?, great view? [*out window*] Hey Mom, go home? [*To them.*] So we're classmates, first-entry-mates? So … do I hug you? Shake your hands? Kiss your hands? Let me move your crate.

[*He moves the crate.*]

COURTNEY/DAPHNE: Thank you./Thanks.

DOUG: Let me center your couch.

[*He moves the couch, grabs his back.*]

DOUG: The backache'll be no problem since I'm already taking aspirin for a pulled thigh. What terrific hair you have, and eyes. The atmosphere of giving and kindness here is contagious?

COURTNEY: Iced tea?

DOUG: Everybody's trying new things? Reaching out? Why iced tea.

COURTNEY: You moved our couch.

DOUG: I've never had iced tea. Why have I never had iced tea. Because, maybe somewhere along the line I was prejudiced? Smelled a skunk out the window and thought: iced tea? So I wrote off iced tea and lived in fear? But now it's time to leave the past behind and have iced tea? [*Out window.*] I'm fine Mom. [*To them.*] The other thing I love here is that no one talks about grades or scores?, they talk about ideas? I wonder if even though on the outside there are so many differences between us, deep down we aren't really all the same?

COURTNEY: Sugar?

DOUG: Sweetheart? Darling? And if even though the individual conforms to society it isn't really society that conforms to the individual in the end? Actually I'll take it plain, here goes?

[*He drinks, grabs a napkin, spits.*]

DOUG: Better head upstairs for another aspirin? [*Starts out, stops.*] Any time you need your refrigerator moved just give a knock? [*Starts out, stops.*] Will you guys be going to the freshmen picnic?

COURTNEY: Surely.

DOUG: Can I juh-juh-juh- ... juh-juh-juh- ... juh-juh-juh- [*Grabs his tongue.*] join you?

COURTNEY: Please do.

[*He goes.*]

COURTNEY: Nice.

DAPHNE: Nice.

COURTNEY: You find him nice?

DAPHNE: You think he's nice, right?

COURTNEY: He moved the crates. He moved the couch. There's no debating it: He's nice.

DAPHNE: Moving the couch hurt his back.

COURTNEY: But he acknowledged it up front.

DAPHNE: Right.

COURTNEY: He can talk about his pain.

DAPHNE: Sensitive.

COURTNEY: Exactly.

DAPHNE: Like Mark and Dave.

COURTNEY: Mark and

DAPHNE: Dave, from my school.

COURTNEY: Did you like Mark and Dave?

DAPHNE: I should have. They were so sensitive.

COURTNEY: With someone this sensitive you could discuss your philosophy.

DAPHNE: Right.

COURTNEY: But if you have concerns about shifting to comp lit or psych, he could discuss your fears.

DAPHNE: Right.

COURTNEY: Or your feelings about your faith ...

DAPHNE: Do I have a faith?

COURTNEY: With him you could find out.

DAPHNE: Any issue.

COURTNEY: But he doesn't just talk.

DAPHNE: Right.

COURTNEY: He identifies a problem, then takes action.

DAPHNE: Aspirin.

COURTNEY: Takes aspirin, takes action, exactly. Which takes courage.

DAPHNE: Right.

COURTNEY: You should go to the picnic together.

DAPHNE: Just the two of us?

COURTNEY: He loved your eyes.

DAPHNE: Both of them.

COURTNEY: I noticed.

DAPHNE: Think he might be ... musical?

COURTNEY: Were Mark and Dave musical?

DAPHNE: Dave played piano.

COURTNEY: This guy might well play piano.

DAPHNE: Jazz?

COURTNEY: I can see him enjoying jazz. Tapping, swaying.

DAPHNE: Can you see us together?

COURTNEY: On the dance floor. Leaning together. Strolling to the punch bowl. A single cup, passed back and forth. He shouts in your ear. You shout in his ear. He grins, you gulp, you dance.

DAPHNE: He enjoys dancing?

COURTNEY: Surely.

DAPHNE: [*Ecstatic.*] At last. [*Suddenly furious.*] God.

COURTNEY: What.

DAPHNE: Why did I let my parents buy me a ticket to fly home over midterm break when I could have had them fly out here.

COURTNEY: To meet Aspirin?

DAPHNE: For once I get a guy who shares dad's love for jazz and I can't bring them together 'til Labor Day when we'd rather be celebrating the end of our first summer living off-campus together with a weekend at the shore.

COURTNEY: Fly home for the Fourth.

DAPHNE: Aspirin'll be seeing his mom.

COURTNEY: If he rearranged crates for you he'll rearrange his schedule for you.

DAPHNE: [*Embracing* COURTNEY.] I'm finally taking off.

[MICHAEL *enters with course cards.*]

MICHAEL: Eight credits from each of groups one and four excluding a writing course other than those in groups two or three unless granted permission by professor, advisor, counselor, or dean. I could fill these out in time for the deadline but I'd rather insert that crate in my nostril. All day I've been feeling so much like a cartoon character that I have to keep pulling my skin to see if it stretches. [*He pulls his lips.*] Human. Hooray. [*He sits.*] So what if this *is* your third choice school, right? You've already survived fifth choice parents on a ninth choice planet. So where are you from? How was your summer? Are you taking blah 101 so you can major in blah, or are you really pre-blah? Will you sign up for blah and go out for the blah or audition for blah? Oh if you went to blah well then you must know blah who I met backpacking through blah on blah.

COURTNEY: Iced tea?

MICHAEL: Why the fuck not.

[*She hands him iced tea. He drinks it all. He looks at them, they look at him.*]

You guys going to the freshman blah blah?

COURTNEY: Surely.

MICHAEL: If I finish my blah should I blah?

COURTNEY: Please do.

[*He goes.*]

DAPHNE: But how will I pull it off.

COURTNEY: It being …

DAPHNE: Dump Aspirin for Course Cards.

COURTNEY: Are you sure that's the move you want to make, at this point in time?

DAPHNE: Jazz with my parents? What was I thinking. That's what I came here to crawl out from under. Aspirin was about to drag me backwards. Til Course Cards snapped his lips and cracked my shell. Allowed me to stop pushing. To let down my smile and accept the quiet. I live to be quiet. I shine when I'm quiet. Did you hear how quiet I was?

COURTNEY: You were quiet.

DAPHNE: I don't want to crush Aspirin. But I can't let him drag me back to my days of Mark and Dave.

COURTNEY: I'll go to the picnic with Aspirin, leaving you free to invite Course Cards.

DAPHNE: Invite …

COURTNEY: March up there, mention you're going, ask him along.

DAPHNE: You really see us together?

COURTNEY: Midnight, late-autumn, two figures, out from the library, across the leaves in slow motion, a few syllables, a few nods, then silence, then a muffin, from his hand, to your lips, to his lips, to his room.

DAPHNE: Raisin?

COURTNEY: What else.

DAPHNE: You don't think he'll mind my cats.

COURTNEY: You have cats?

DAPHNE: I hope to. Someday.

COURTNEY: They'll curl up on his lap as he watches his cartoons.

DAPHNE: [*Embracing* COURTNEY.] I'm finally moving on.

COURTNEY: But before heading up, I'd change out of school colors.

DAPHNE: School colors.

COURTNEY: On your top.

DAPHNE: These aren't school colors.

COURTNEY: Close enough.

DAPHNE: [*Gasps.*]

COURTNEY: For your tryst with Course Cards, you'll want to steer clear of school colors.

DAPHNE: He caught me in school colors.

COURTNEY: We'll erase the mis-impression from his mind … as I dig deep into my trunk, and cloak you in black.

DAPHNE: Black. [*Thinks.*] You saved my life.

[COURTNEY *goes into the bedroom.* DAPHNE *goes to the phone, makes a call.*]

DAPHNE: Pick up. I'm here. It's great. I won't be home for break. Call

me. I won't be home this summer, I'm free, I'm flying, I can see ...
everything, all your crap, what *was* that. Call me I'll explain. You won't
get it, how could you. You're so old. I've gone a million miles,
you're staying still. You'll never get it. You'll never reach me. Call
me.

[DAPHNE *hangs up, moves around.* DOUG *enters.*]

DOUG: Everybody's starting to mingle in these little clusters?, The
chicken smells great?

DAPHNE: I'm not going.

DOUG: Thank you for having the courage to stand up, to something so
obligatory, so unnecessary, so how was your summer?

DAPHNE: I'll drop in on the picnic later.

DOUG: You're right, let the others break the ice? Your roommate already
went but who cares, you're the one with the eyes, beautiful eyes? Did
you like high school?

DAPHNE: Did I ...

DOUG: A haze? Mine too?

DAPHNE: I need some time ...

DOUG: So do I, before we go?

DAPHNE: Please let me finish my sentence.

DOUG: We're finishing each other's sentences? What does that say?

DAPHNE: Nothing.

DOUG: You're right, but as nothing was being said, what really happened?

DAPHNE: Time passed.

DOUG: Time passed, you're right, so I guess we should go?

DAPHNE: I have plans. But my roommate will go to the picnic with you when she's ready.

DOUG: Just me and her? Her hair lights up a room. It would be wonderful if she would hurry because my roommate's coming down and he has this tendency to whine that the earth is his ninth choice planet?

DAPHNE: That's your roommate?

DOUG: I like him and I think he's great but he's always breathing on people and tagging along?, I tried to slip out while he was doing his course cards but when he heard my plans he said he'd be right down?

[DAPHNE *hurries into the bedroom.*]

DAPHNE: Course Cards'll be right down.

COURTNEY: Here's your outfit.

[DOUG *follows* DAPHNE *into the bedroom.*]

DAPHNE: I need to change.

DOUG: Who reads Joyce? I love Joyce. Who collects stuffed animals?

[DAPHNE *hurries out from the bedroom into the living room, closing the bedroom door behind her.*]

DOUG: [*Behind door.*] Who closed the door?

[DAPHNE *starts frantically changing her clothes.*]

DOUG: [*Behind door, to* COURTNEY.] I'll wait out there 'til you're ready? [DOUG *hurries out of the bedroom, closing the bedroom door behind him, sees* DAPHNE *undressed, stands frozen.*] I don't have any sisters but my cousins are girls?

[DAPHNE *goes into the livingroom closet, closes the door.* DOUG *paces.*]

DAPHNE: [*From closet.*] You've got me in short sleeves.

COURTNEY: [*From room.*] It's still summer.

DAPHNE: [*From closet.*] I hate my arms.

COURTNEY: [*From room.*] Your arms are great.

DOUG: My birthday's September fifteenth?

[*There's a knock on the main door.*]

[*To himself.*] Here he is to tag along on my date. [DOUG *charges to the bedroom door, knocks.*]

COURTNEY & DAPHNE: [*From bedroom and closet.*] Come in.

[DOUG *slips into the bedroom, closing the door behind him.* MICHAEL *enters the living room, closing the door behind him.*]

[DAPHNE *steps out of the closet dressed in black.*]

DAPHNE: Fifth choice parents on a ninth choice planet. I love what you said. I'd been, wrestling with, something, and the minute you said it I thought, that's it.

MICHAEL: [*No response.*]

DAPHNE: We don't choose our parents. We don't choose our planet.

MICHAEL: [*No response.*]

DAPHNE: So there's this ... odd ...

MICHAEL: Actually I'm very close with my parents.

DAPHNE: Yeah.

MICHAEL: I visit my dad. He's gotten it together.

DAPHNE: Right.

MICHAEL: I laugh with his wife. I tickle their babies.

DAPHNE: Right.

MICHAEL: I drop in on mom. Say hi to her husband. Keep up with with his kids. Say hi to my brothers.

DAPHNE: Yeah.

MICHAEL: I'm back in touch with mom's ex. My sister stays in his basement.

DAPHNE: Uh huh. But I mean, this sort of —

MICHAEL: I'm very close with this planet too.

DAPHNE: Right.

MICHAEL: Air. Water. Great location.

DAPHNE: Right.

MICHAEL: Me and my planet, two heaps of shit going in circles.

DAPHNE: But moving in here, you feel this sort of —

[*A sudden sound from inside the bedroom.*]

DAPHNE: You know because it's all so —

[*From the bedroom, sounds of bed rocking. Gasps, groans, grunts. Silence.*]

DAPHNE: It's all sort of —

[COURTNEY *rushes out, wrapped in towel, hurries through livingroom and out main door [to the bathroom]. Sound of running water.*]

DAPHNE: I ...

[DOUG *rushes out, wrapped in towel, hurries through livingroom and out main door [to the bathroom]. Sound of running water.*]

DAPHNE: I ...

[COURTNEY *charges back through main door, into bedroom, closing doors behind her.* DOUG *charges back through main door, into bedroom, closing doors behind him.* DAPHNE *charges into closet.* MICHAEL *sits there.* DOUG *comes out from the bedroom, dishevelled, despondent, closes the door behind him, sits.*]

DOUG: No one here knows my high school hike club scaled four peaks, I led the way, I won a prize. No one here knows I sprained my foot in a snake pit, kept right on going, everybody cheered and elected me president. No one here knows the feeling, your boots in the dirt, your face in the wind, your picture in the paper. What a gang, what a time, no one knows.

MICHAEL: About ready to head to the picnic?

DOUG: I might have a prior commitment.

MICHAEL: If you had a prior commitment, you'd already know.

DOUG: She'll be right out, to let me know.

MICHAEL: If you want her to want you, don't let her catch you waiting for her.

DOUG: [*Looks to the bedroom door, thinks.*] Huh.

MICHAEL: You might also want to go for some deodorant.

DOUG: I go for plenty of deodorant.

MICHAEL: Go for more.

DOUG: [*Sniffs himself, thinks.*] Huh.

MICHAEL: Let's head up to the room. I'll do course cards, you call about your lab course …

DOUG: Why are you telling me to call about my lab course?

MICHAEL: To see if you're in.

DOUG: I did see. I'm … almost in.

MICHAEL: Almost in?

DOUG: If someone drops out, I'm in.

MICHAEL: Oh.

DOUG: [*Suddenly incensed.*] Excuse me but I'm proud of being almost in? Okay "almost in" is a key step towards being in? Okay I'm sorry I'm not as "in" as you think humanly necessary but not everybody was born into a nationally ranked program that basically guarantees advanced standing?, but at least I'm sticking out my neck instead of dreaming about some graduate level seminar while fiddling with my god damn course cards?

[DOUG *charges out the main door.* DAPHNE *steps out from the closet.*]

DAPHNE: [*To* MICHAEL.] I'm heading out if you want to come …

[COURTNEY *comes out of the bedroom.*]

COURTNEY: If I joined you two, would that be okay?

DAPHNE: Might it not be not okay for you?

COURTNEY: It'll be great for me, as long as it's okay with you.

DAPHNE: But, might you not, see something better, and feel tied?

COURTNEY: No.

DAPHNE: But aren't you always keeping an eye out, for, you know, whatever, whatever else?

COURTNEY: When things happen, things happen, but, I never lose sight of my friends. How can you say that.

DAPHNE: I meant that crate to be for my books, so why is it covered with your candles?

COURTNEY: When you tacitly approve of someone's candles on your crate while secretly resenting them, you're not doing the person a favor.

[DOUG *enters with flowers.*]

DOUG: [*To* COURTNEY.] What was I doing standing in the flowers being stared at like I was crazy by the people I'd been talking with almost happily 'til the wind shifted and filled me with this feeling of your hair that swept fingers to flowers and feet to stairs to invite you to join me, please join me?

COURTNEY: I'm so sorry, but my roommate and I are in the middle of a conversation.

DAPHNE: [*To* MICHAEL.] Weren't *we* in the middle of a conversation?

DOUG: Where's the god damned iced tea.

COURTNEY: It's empty.

DOUG: I want another crack at it, just one more crack.

COURTNEY: I'm sorry.

24   BILLY ARONSON

[*The phone starts ringing.*]

DOUG: I'll re-center your couch. I'll flip it around. I'll stand it on its legs.

COURTNEY: I'm sorry.

DOUG: [*On his back, beneath couch.*] Did I only *dream* you wanted to go to the picnic with me? [*To* DAPHNE.] If you had other plans what happened to them?

DAPHNE: [*Not moving.*] I'm going to take a nap.

COURTNEY: [*To* MICHAEL.] Have you any idea how absolutely rude it is to sit there, as though we're not worth one syllable of your divine wisdom?

[DAPHNE *picks up the receiver.*]

DAPHNE: Oh hi. Right. [*Pause.*] Right. [*Pause.*] [*She hangs up.*]

DAPHNE: My father died.

[*Everybody stands there. Blackout.*]

END OF PLAY

Pearl Cleage

CHAIN

Pearl Cleage

Pearl Cleage is an Atlanta based writer whose most recent novel, *What Looks Like Crazy On An Ordinary Day*, became a *New York Times* Bestseller and was chosen as part of Oprah's Book Club. Other recent works include *Blues for An Alabama Sky*, a full-length drama commissioned and premiered at The Alliance Theatre in 1995, under the direction of Kenny Leon. *Blues* returned to Atlanta as part of the 1996 Olympic Games following a production at Hartford Stage and broke attendance records at Arena Stage in Washington, D.C.

Cleage is also the author of *Flyin' West*, a full-length drama commissioned and premiered at The Alliance Theatre in 1992. *Deals With the Devil and Other Reasons to Riot*, a book of essays published by Ballantine/One World in 1993, and *MAD AT MILES: A Black Woman's Guide to Truth*, published by the Cleage Group in 1991. Her play, *Bourbon at the Border*, was produced at The Alliance Theatre in April of 1997. Her first novel, *Tunnels of Love*, was published by Avon Books.

Since opening at The Alliance Theatre under the direction of Kenny Leon, *Flyin' West* has had more than a dozen productions across the country, including The Kennedy Center in Washington, D.C., The Brooklyn Academy of Music, The Indiana Repertory Company, Crossroads Theatre Company, The Alabama Shakespeare Festival, The Intiman Theatre in Seattle, Washington, The St. Louis Black Repertory Theatre, and The Long Wharf Theatre, making it one of the most produced new plays in the country for 1994.

Pearl is also a regular columnist for *The Atlanta Tribune*, a contributing editor of *Ms. Magazine* and a regular contributor to *Essence Magazine*. Her work has also appeared in numerous anthologies, including: *Double Stitch*, *Black Drama in America*, *New Play's From the Woman's Project*, and *Contemporary Plays by Women of Color*, Pearl is an artistic associate of Just Us Theatre Company in Atlanta and founding editor of *CATALYST*, a magazine of heart and mind.

Pearl is the mother of one daughter, Deignan, and the wife of novelist, Zaron W. Burnett, Jr.

CHARACTERS

ROSA JENKINS, *a 16 year old black girl, addicted to crack.*

SETTING: *A one bedroom apartment in a battered Harlem, New York apartment building.*

TIME: *1991*

DAY ONE

The stage and the house are completely dark. A SLIDE comes up on a screen at the rear of the stage: DAY ONE. The slide holds for ten seconds and then disappears, leaving us again in complete darkness. The sounds that we can hear should come from this darkness suddenly, starting with a loud scream. There are sounds of scuffling, struggling, trying to escape and being caught. Only one voice is heard, the voice of ROSA JENKINS, a 16-year-old crack addict. It should be clear that there is a struggle going on, but the cause of the struggle should be completely unknown, adding to the frightening nature of the sounds.

ROSA: [*Screaming, crying, pleading in the darkness.*] What are you doing? No! Stop It!! Don't, Daddy!! Please don't!! Stop it!! Stop it! Daddy, don't do that! Please don't do that!! Daddy! Daddy! Wait, Daddy!! Wait! Don't do it! Please, don't do it! Daddy, Please! Please!

[*The sounds of struggle suddenly stop, but the loud sobbing continues. There is the sound of footsteps and then the sound of a door slamming and a deadbolt lock clicking loudly into place. Silence, suddenly broken by ROSA's shriek.*]

ROSA: Da-a-a-a-a-deeeeee!!

[*Lights up full. ROSA is crumpled in a heap in the middle of the floor. She is sobbing loudly. The apartment around her is small and crowded with well worn furniture, a television set, plastic fruit or flowers, a cheaply framed picture of John Kennedy, Martin Luther King and Bobby Kennedy. Another framed dime store painting of a white Jesus.*
ROSA cries bitterly for a few minutes, then she sits up suddenly.]

ROSA: Mama? [*She listens intently and then speaks tentatively.*] Mama? Is that you? [*Listens again and then speaks angrily.*] I hear you out there listening. What kind of mother are you? How can you let him do this to me? You don't love me! You never loved me!! You hate me! You all hate me!! [*Crumples again, sobbing. Stops suddenly and sits up. This time her look is more crafty. She is still listening.*] Mama? Mama are you still there? I didn't mean it, Mama. You know I didn't mean it. I know you love me. It's me. I know it's me. I love you, Mama. [*Listens.*] Mama? Can you hear me? I know you can hear me. I can hear you breathing! Talk to me, Mama. Say something. Say anything!! [*Angry again.*] Well, don't then! I don't care what you do! You can't keep me in here if I don't want to stay! I'll get away just like I always do. You know I can do it, Mama!! And you know I will! So you might as well go on to work and stop waiting to see what I'm gonna do. I'm gonna do what I damn well please and there's nothing you can do about it. Not a goddamn thing!! Now!! How do you like that? [*Listens again. Suddenly frightened.*] Mama? Please let me out! I'm scared to be in here like this! Please let me out, Mama! I won't tell Daddy, I promise. He'll never know the difference. I won't go nowhere, I swear. I was just kiddin'. You can trust me, Mama. Honest! [*No sound at aft from outside. She is suddenly enraged.*] Open this door and look at me! You scared to see me like this? [*Laughs crazily.*] Well, that's just too damn bad because you gotta deal with it. Look at me!

[ROSA *lunges for the door and for the first time we see that she is chained to the radiator with a long, thick chain. The chain is about six feet long and strong enough to hold her. She is shackled by her left foot. The chain is long enough for her to have some range of motion, but not long enough for her to get to the door. As she lunges toward it, the chain jerks her back, twisting her ankle painfully. She yelps in pain and falls down again. She grabs the chain and tries to pull it off of her leg, but she can't. She goes to the radiator and tries to pull the chain off of the radiator, but she can't. She becomes more and more frantic as she pulls on it futilely. She is like a caged animal and she growls in her throat in a way that expresses wordless rage and frustration. She paces around the apartment as the reality of what has happened settles on her. She is wild. Almost out of control. She pulls on the chain, shakes it, rattles it, etc. She stands breathlessly looking around at the apartment. Suddenly, she grabs a portrait of her mother and father and herself at a younger age and throws it to the ground. The glass in the frame shatters against the floor and the noise seems to dissipate her rage. She collapses near the glass fragments, weeping loudly. After a minute, she sits up and looks at the glass. She picks up a large shard and, still weeping, holds it over her wrist. She slowly tries to bring it down across her arm, but she doesn't have the nerve. She holds it trembling there for a long moment and then throws it away and collapses in a silent heap on the floor.*]

[*Black. Lights up.*]

[ROSA *is searching through the house as far as her chain will allow her movement. She is moving awkwardly. She tangles the chain in things, stumbles over it, etc.*]

ROSA: [*Jerking the chain angrily.*] Damn!

[*She flops down on the sofa, frustrated and angry. She is facing the audience and seems to see them for the first time. Her face is startled, but almost immediately takes on the craftiness of the dope fiend.*]

ROSA: Got a match? [*She holds up a wrinkled cigarette.*] Hey! I'm talking to you! Y'all got a match? [*Disgusted at the lack of response.*] It ain't no reefer, okay? It's a Winston or some shit. [*A beat.*] Oh, I see. I'm invisible, right? You looking right at me and nobody see me, right? Okay. No problem. [*A beat.*] Y'all probably don't smoke no way. Right? Lookin out for your health and shit. You probably wouldn't give me a damn match if you had it. [*A beat*] My dad told you not to talk to me, right? Not to listen to anything I said cuz I'm a dope fiend and I might trick you into doing something bad.

Fuck it. [*She tosses cigarette aside. Throughout her talking she moves restlessly around. She touches the chain a lot because the awkwardness and horror make it impossible for her to keep her hands off of it. She is also a dope fiend and she is already feeling the effects of being deprived of the drug.*]

These country ass niggas think they can keep me chained up in here like some kind of freak. But that's where they wrong. I ain't no dumb ass dog! I can figure this shit out. Be back on the street before they country asses get home from work tonight.

I wasted a lot of time yesterday cause I was in a state of shock or some shit. I couldn't believe this shit was really happening to me. Of all people! Now I know I have been kind of crazy lately, but this shit … this is like some movie of the week shit, here. Geraldo and shit. I mean, when I got home, they was actin so glad to see me and shit and now this?

My Dad just gave the guy the money without talking a whole lot of bullshit about what he was gonna do if they didn't leave me alone and shit. Now even I was surprised at that. He used to go off! Hollerin and shit. Talkin about callin the cops and turnin everybody in. Next time I'd get loose and come around, nobody wanted to let me in cause they were scared my pops was gonna come back and turn out.

He would, too. Every damn time. Them niggas used to crack up behind that shit, too. My Dad would start tellin them how they ought to be ashamed to be sellin that shit to kids and wasn't nobody in there more than 17. Buyin or sellin! He didn't do it this time though. I guess he was just tired of the shit.

Or he was tryin to throw me off. Make me think he wadn't gonna do nothin and then wham! Here come this shit! I slept all day Saturday. I been up for three days. Maybe four. Next morning ... before they went to work, I came out to tell 'em good-by and they sittin at the table talkin real quiet and they stop real fast when I come in. Then they look at each other and my dad pulls out a chair for me. They was lookin so serious, I thought they was gettin' ready to send me back to rehab and then my dad goes to the closet and pulls out this big ass bag and comes over and sits down beside me and hugs me and shit and starts talking about how happy they were when I was first born and shit and how I'll always be their daughter and they love me so much and I'm thinkin', yeah, okay for this Father knows Best crap, but what's in the damn bag? Then I looked at Mama and she's cryin' and shit.

Mama ain't cried when I went to rehab since I was thirteen, so I know this is some serious shit. I know this sounds crazy, but I thought they was gonna kill me. I could tell it was something heavy in the bag and I thought maybe Daddy had, like a sledge hammer, or something and they was gonna beat me to death and then put me in a bag and drop me in the river. [*Laughs.*] Crazy shit, right? But you know your mind give you all kinda shit when you get scared.

Then Daddy takes out this big ass chain and shit and I freaked. I started running around the room and I tried to hold onto Mama and she was holding me and we was both crying. Look like The Color Purple and shit. "Save me, Mama! Save me!" But that shit didn't work on Daddy no better than it did that nigga in the movie. He pulled my hands offa her and made her go on to work. She didn't want to go and I was screaming and crying and begging her not to do this to me and she was crying, too, but Daddy was holding me so tight I could hardly breathe and he kept talking to Mama in this very calm voice and reminding her that they had talked about this and telling her that this was the only way and it was for my own good. Shit like that. So she looked at me and then she grabbed her purse and ran out the room. Then it was just me and daddy.

[*She picks up the cigarette again.*]

I know one of y'all got a damn match. I swear this is a Winston. If it was some reefer I'd eat it, okay? [*A beat.*] Fuck it. I hate cigarettes anyway. My junior high school teacher used to catch us smokin in the bathroom and make us flush them down the toilet. I didn't care. I was just doin' it cause Paula was doin it and she my girl. A nasty habit, that's what Miss Young would say. Smoking is a nasty habit!

Paula say smokin ain't nothin. She can tell the bitch about a couple of sho nuff nasty habits if she, really interested. [*Laughing.*] Paula would do that shit, too. She crazy. She say anything to people and just walk away. Most of the time they too surprised to say anything back or they just start laughing. I can't do that shit. If I say some smart ass shit to people they wanna fight. That's cause she cute. They don't care what she say cause they like lookin at her while she standin there sayin it.

[*She touches the chain and jumps, having forgotten it for a minute.*]

I told Paula she better stop smoking cause she pregnant now and that shit make your baby come out real little and be sick all the time. She say she gave up smokin reefer 'til the nigga born. She ain't givin up nothing else. Then she roll her eyes and wink like she know somethin I don't know. I ask her do she mean her and Darryl still fuckin, big as her stomach done got and she say that is a personal question, which mean yes! Paula a freak anyway, though, so you never can tell. I told her she don't ever need to start smoking no rock cause she would be a coke hoe in about ten seconds.

[*Laughs.*]

Me and her used to smoke a lot of reefer together when we was in seventh grade. Miss Young's class. She used to read to us at the end of the day right before we went home and I'd be so high, Paula had to keep wakin me up about every two seconds.

A lotta people like they reefer, but I'm not down wit it. I figure, what's the point? If I'm gonna go to all the trouble to get some money and go buy some shit, I wanna get as high as I can. I don't want to be somewhere sleep with my mouth all open and shit. I want to be awake so I can feel something!

[*Looking around, disgusted.*]

They didn't even leave the t.v. in here. One of those tight ass blond bitches at my last drug rehab told my mom that she thought maybe watching t.v. was "overstimulating" me and making me wanna do drugs. And my moms went for it! Made me stop watchin t.v., except for The Cosby Show cause she think the Cosby kids are role models and shit. Yeah, right. Put my ass in a great big house with a whole lotta money and I'll be a role model, too.

I tried to tell her that t.v. ain't shit stimulation compared to what's up on the street! It's always somethin happenin out there. They just don't see it. Or they see it and they scared of it. I ain't scared of nothin. I seen more shit in sixteen years than they seen in forty and I know how to handle it. Jesus [*NOTE: His name is pronounced in Spanish —* "*Hey-suess*"] say you either gotto get into it or it's gonna get into you. [*A beat.*] No. What he says is if it's gonna get into you, you gotta get into ... no. Wait. [*A beat.*] If it gets ... [*A beat.*] Fuck it. It sounds like it makes sense when he say it, but I can't get that shit straight. [*A beat.*] I feel like shit. [*A beat, then louder*] I feel like shit! [*A beat.*] And don't nobody give a fuck. They say they do, but they really don't. Otherwise, [*This rises to a shriek by the end of the sentence.*] they would leave me the fuck alone and bring me some damn rock up in here so I can get high! [*A beat.*] Always tellin me how hard life is. Didn't nobody tell them to be workin at Harlem Hospital every damn day of the week.

[*A beat.*]

They never would have found me if Jesus hadn't a told, with his ignorant "I'll be right back" ass. Nobody else knew where I was to be sendin somebody bustin up in the place. No reason to. Daddy hadn't offered no reward. "Have you seen this girl? Twenty five dollar reward." Goddam crack addicts will turn your ass in for a quarter so muthafuckas got signs all over the neighborhood. People be turnin in they friends and shit. Ain't no crack addict gonna keep no secret if there's dope money comin from tellin' it. If my daddy had offered a reward, I'd a turned myself in! Shit!

I figure ain't nobody got more of a right to collect a reward on somebody than that same somebody, right?

[*Forgetting the chain, she rises and heads for the kitchen. The chain jerks her back.*]

Damn! [*Rising anger.*] Damn! [*She sits again, drawing up her knees and rocking back and forth with some agitation. She really wants some crack. She suddenly sees some matches under the couch. She drags the chain awkwardly over and finally reaches them with great effort. She sits on the floor exhausted and lights the Winston. She inhales deeply and then explodes into a terrible cough. She cannot get her breath for several seconds. When she regains her composure, she takes a deep breath and looks around. She snubs out the Winston and begins to crumble. She hugs her knees to her chest, bows her head and begins to rock silently back and forth.*]

[*Black.*]

[*Slide up: DAY THREE*]

[ROSA *is trying to sleep on the couch under a child's worn bedspread with colorful cartoon figures on it. She tosses fitfully, but can't figure out a way to sleep comfortably with the chain on her leg. She sits up in frustration.*]

ROSA: Help! [*She waits. Listens. Then louder.*] Help!! [*Listening.*] Help, they're killin me! [*Listens.*] Yeah, right. Niggas run the other way when they hear that shit. [*Thinks for a minute.*] Fire! [*Listens. Still nothing.*] Shit I could burn up and nobody would even know I was in this muthafucka. I ought to have them arrested for doing this to me. [*A beat.*] I wonder if I really could … Daddy would kill me! [*A beat.*] He couldn't kill me! His ass would be in jail. That would kill Mama. Shit!

Maybe Jesus will rescue me. That'd be some shit he would do. Come busting up in here with the Fire Department and shit. I'd be out before Mama and Daddy even got home!

Jesus ain't gonna do no shit like that. He probably figurin I'll get out this time just like I been gettin out before. He don't know nothin about no chain. He probably figure they sent me down south again. Naw, he know that ain't happenin. [*Laughs.*] They ain't looking to see Rosa Jenkins no time soon in Alabama. Country ass niggas. Tellin me how worried my Mama was about me and what a good girl they knew I still was underneath. Yeah, right. I hate when people are so stupid they just make you take their shit. You know, like before you got there, they was on the honor system and shit, cause they in Alabama. I know they act like I killed somebody when I tried to cash one of grandmomma's social security checks. It ain't like the government won't replace that shit! If you tell em somebody stole your check, they send you another one. People up here do it all the time. I didn't think that shit was no big deal, but the man at the store knew my grandmother and he called her and told her I'd been there with her check and he had cashed it this time, but could she please send a note the next time. My grandmother just thanked him and said she would, but when I got home she had called my uncle for back-up and they both went off on me. Both of them! I had never heard my grandmother talk so much shit. I thought they were goin to have me arrested and shit, but they didn't. They just sent me back up here.

My grandmother hates to hear me cuss. She heard me on the phone once talking long distance to one of my friends. It might have been Jesus, I don't remember, but I was talking … like I talk. My grandmother took that phone and said: "I apologize for my grandaughter's language. She did not learn how to talk like that in this house." And she hung up the phone and took me in the bathroom and washed my mouth out with Ivory soap. I was almost fifteen years old, but grandmothers don't care about your real age. They got a age they want you to be and that is the age you gonna be when they around you. My grandmother age ain't but ten. That's how old I was the summer we moved up here, and she can't get past it. I was ten then, and to her, I'm gonna be ten. She heard all those muthafuckas coming out of my mouth and she just couldn't handle it.

Nobody talks like this in Tuskegee. They cuss and shit, but not like in New York. Everybody in New York cuss all the time. When they happy, when they mad. They just be cussin. The first day we moved on this block, I was sittin on the stoop out front while Daddy moved our stuff inside and I was looking at this guy staggerin down the street, bumpin into people and shit. I had never seen anybody that drunk before, so I was starin at him, with my country ass, and he saw me doin it. Cussed me out! [*Laughs.*] what the fuck you looking at?

He hollered right in my face. I like died!

New York is so different from Alabama it might as well be on another planet or some shit. When we got here, I was freaked out. I had never even been to Montgomery, except once on a church bus when I was three. My parents call themselves movin to New York so I could go to good schools and have better opportunities and shit. Yeah, right. Opportunities to do what?

I ain't complainin though. It was exciting as hell. I had never seen kids my age do the shit these New York niggas were doing. They did everything. I mean eleven, twelve year old kids drinkin and smokin and fuckin like they was grown already. It was like nobody had control of them or somethin.

I didn't do none of that shit for a long time. I was real goody goody. The kids at my school used to call me "Bama and shit and make fun of me because I wadn't down with the shit they knew from birth or some shit. It was kind of a drag at first, but then I met Jesus and he hipped me to a lot of shit about living in New York. Stuff I really needed to know, right? And plus, he was real fine and real cool and a Puerto Rican. Wadn't one Puerto Rican in Tuskegee, Alabama. Period. He thought I was Puerto Rican before he met me because my name was Rosa and some nigga told him I had a accent. He thought they meant a Spanish accent, but they was talkin about a Alabama accent. He thought that shit was real funny, too. Pissed me off 'til I saw he didn't mean nothin by it.

See, it wadn't about me. Jesus thought everything was funny. Not the regular stuff you'd think somebody'd laugh at. A lot of weird shit. Like he thought it was funny that my parents had come here so we would have a better life. And look at ëem now, he says. They got shitty ass jobs and a crack head kid. He thought that was real funny. Jesus parents came all the way from Puerto Rico. Well, his mother did. He never said nothin about his father and I never did ask him. People in Alabama ask you your life story if they sit next to you on the bus, but people in New York don't play that shit.

My parents used to do all that tourist shit when we first got here. They walked my little ass all over New York city lookin at shit that was supposed to make you go "O-o-o-o-o, shit! New York City! Ain't this a bitch?" It's like that Stevie Wonder oldie where the country ass guy gets off the bus and says "New York City! Skyscrapers and everything!" And then the New York niggas take everything he got! [*She laughs.*]

We went to see The Statue of Liberty and shit. Everybody

standing around there looking at it like it mean something and this guy with a uniform and shit tell you about how old it is and how they got it and shit and you can tell he say this shit twenty-five times a day cause he don't even look at you while he talkin. He just be talkin. If you wanna listen, fine. If you don't, that's fine, too. He's gettin' paid to say that shit, not to make you listen. Muthafucka shoulda been a teacher! [*Laughs.*]

Jesus' momma was scared to take him a lotta places cause she didn't speak English too good yet. So he been here since he was five and he still ain't never seen the Statue of Liberty. I told him we should get high and go down there one day and listen to that guy say his shit. Jesus momma look like that woman in West Side. The one with the purple dress and the fine boyfriend? Jesus like to look at the video cause it make him think about his momma. Jesus don't look like that, though. He ain't that kinda Puerto Rican. He look just like a nigga, in fact. I always thought Puerto Ricans looked like Mexicans or some shit, but a lot of them look just like niggas. Maybe there was some Country ass Puerto Ricans in Tuskegee and I just didn't recognize em.

Ain't nothin country about Jesus. He hard about shit. Not that he mean or nothin, not to me, anyway, but don't nothin fuck with him. He can look at terrible shit and, just walk away. He won't even blink. We saw a kid we knew get blown away one time. He owed some people money and he had been talkin around bout how he wasn't payin shit so they came up to the school and waited for him. When he came out the front door, they jumped out the car, shot his ass and drove the fuck away, cool as shit. Everybody freaked. Runnin and screamin and shit. Jesus didn't even jump. He just kept walkin. It was scary unless you was wit him. Then it made you feel good. Like whatever happen, it ain't gonna be no surprise to this nigga.

I think it was because he had seen such terrible shit already, you know? That's how he started smokin rock in the first place, behind some really terrible shit. Shit like you would hear about, but not know anybody who been through it personally. Well, Jesus had some of that shit happen to him. [*A beat, then a shrug.*] He don't care if I tell it … and I don't owe him shit any damn way!

Jesus mama had a boyfriend, right? And the nigga was a crack-head and she hid his shit from him. Call herself tryin to help him get off it. Well, she wouldn't tell him where the shit was, so he shot her right there in their apartment, went through all her shit until he found it, and was sittin there smokin it when Jesus came home. Jesus mama layin right on the floor in the next room, dead as shit, and this nigga so high he don't even give a fuck. Jesus say the nigga didn't even tell him she was dead. He just looked up when he walked in and said, "Your mama in the kitchen." When he came back out, the nigga was gone. [*A beat.*] I told you it was some terrible shit.

So after they buried her and shit, Jesus said he started thinkin about that nigga just sittin there smokin while his mama layin in the next room dead and he said he just thought, well, fuck it. If the shit that damn good, let me have it. I told him he was just thinkin that way cause he felt bad about his mom and shit, but he said he wadn't askin me if he should do it. He was just tellin me.

He didn't act like no addict either. He don't act like one now, unless he can't get the shit, then he start actin weird. Talkin crazy and shit. When Jesus need to get high, he talk about killin people a lot. He ain't never killed nobody, but he talk about that shit a lot when he can't get high. I know it's because of his mama, so I try to change the subject so he won't go off on it. Paula be scared of Jesus when he talk that shit, but she ain't know him as long as I have. I been knowin Jesus since I was eleven years old. How he gonna scare me after all that?

I don't think I woulda started smoking this shit if it wadn't for Jesus. It didn't seem to be doin' nothin so bad to him and he was sellin it so he always had some. Plus, he still had the apartment from his mom's insurance, so he didn't have to go to no crack house or nothin to get high. He could just kick back at his own crib.

But then he told me it made people nervous for me to be around so much if I wadn't gonna be smokin. They was telling him I was fuckin up their high. People thought I might be a cop of some shit. That's cause niggas watch too much t.v. Like the cops really gonna hire somebody to live in the neighborhood undercover, right? They gonna train me to spy on a bunch of poor ass niggas don't nobody care about no way. But niggas are so paranoid, they believe that shit. I actually heard two niggas talkin about whether or not I was a undercover cop and one of them said no because anybody the cops used undercover had to be fine. It made me mad as hell, and then I said, Rosa! You goin' off on some shit you overheard a crack addict say. What is wrong with you, girl? But I didn't like hearin that kinda shit just cause — I I — wadn't down wit it. So, I said okay, fuck it.

And that shit is good. I am not lying. I mean if you like to get high, it will get you high real fast. Now some people ain't down wit it, and that's cool, but if you wanna get high, that rock is the shit. I mean, it feel so good, you don't care where you are, what you look

like, what is happenin to the other niggas in the room or any of that
shit. You just feel good. And like in a real personal way. It ain't like
you need nobody else to feel good with you. You feel so good, your
own high be keepin you company.

[*A beat.*]

   The only problem is that shit don't last long. And once you feel
that good, you gotta feel that good again, right? I mean, why wouldn't
you? You gotta want something. Rock good as anything else you gonna
want. And if you careful, you can handle that shit and not let it handle you.
   See, my daddy got this old timey attitude that if he don't like it,
I'm not spose to like it. And since he don't smoke no rock, I'm not
spose to smoke none either. I wish my dad would get high one time.
I'll bet he would be a funny muthafucka. With his country ass. My
dad don't even drink nothin but beer! My mom don't drink shit. So
they don't know what the fuck I'm even talkin about. They brought
me all these pamphlets and shit — "Just say no!" What the fuck does
that mean?
   I used to think my dad knew everything. But you can't know everything about New York City. Not even about Harlem. Not even this
one block in Harlem! When I was gone a whole week, I wadn't two
buildings down from here. I used to watch my mom and dad out the
window. I saw em asking who had seen me and shit. Half the niggas
they asked had been smokin with me half the night! They didn't give
a fuck.
   My Dad wanted to kill Jesus when he found out I was smokin it,
but I won't tell him where Jesus live. He act like it's Jesus' fault I'm
smokin it. Say this shit about if Jesus was really my "friend" he
wouldn't give me that shit. [*Laughs.*] I told you my dad be trippin!
He never did like me to be around Jesus after what happen to Jesus
mom. I told him that wadn't none of Jesus fault, but my dad didn't
wanna hear that shit. Jesus had his own place so my dad thought I'd
be over there all the time fuckin and shit. I don't even think he
thought about me gettin high. He just didn't want me to be fuckin.
   [*Laughs.*] Jesus place was usually so full of crack heads wadn't no
place to be fuckin if we wanted to. Jesus didn't care nothin bout that
no way. I don't know why. I think all of Jesus weird shit is because
of how that shit went down with his moms. But I know he didn't care
nothin about it cause I used to try to get him to do it with me, and he

wouldn't. Jesus like to get high. Everything else is take it or leave it. I think that's why he wanted me to start smokin rock, too. He wanted us to do it together. Romantic and shit, right? [*Laughs.*] He always used to tell me he just wadn't down wit no whole lot of fuckin, but that if I wanted to do it with somebody else, he wouldn't be pissed off or nothin. Well, that wadn't what I wanted, so I kept bringin it up and bringin it up and finally he said he would teach me how to do somethin that he like to watch. And I said okay ...

At first I thought I could do it in here to pass the time, right? I mean no t.v. No Nintendo. No telephone. Shit! But I can't do it if nobody ain't watching me. I don't know why. I guess I'm as big a freak as Paula, with her pregnant ass.

Sometimes when we needed money, he'd get me to do it in front of some niggas. They thought it was funny that I could get off like that and still be a virgin. It was just Jesus watchin me, I guess. He'd be lookin right in my face, too. I'd be goin off and he just be lookin' at me, thinkin about gettin high, calm as shit. He said he used to hear his mother and father fuckin when he was real little and sometimes he'd pretend his mother was doin' it with him instead of his father. I told him not to tell me none of that freak Puerto Rican shit!

I love to hear jesus say my name like it was Spanish. "R-r-r-r-r-r-rosa!" He rolls that "r" around so long I can't stand it. Shit sound like rollin lemon heads around in your mouth. If I was doin it and he called my name like that, I'd get off in a second. When it was somebody I didn't want to do it in front of, he would tell me to just listen for my name and it would be easy. He wadn't lyin either. Worked every time.

[*A beat.*]

Last night when they got home, my Mom was still cryin and shit. They had both worked double shift, too, so it was late and they was good and worried about how I was gonna be when they got here. I started to lay out like I was dead so when they opened the door they'd see me layin there with my eyes open and shit. But I knew that would really fuck with them and I didn't want my daddy to go off. So I was just sittin here when they busted in all hyper and shit. My Mom started huggin me and my Dad was lookin real relieved and shit and it seemed like they were surprised to see me still there, right? They were scared I had figured a way to get out and wouldn't nothin be here but the goddam chain. No Rosa! Well, they was wrong this time, but they gonna be right pretty soon.

I shoulda asked them how they figure I could get away, but I know they wouldn't tell me. They did unchain my ass while they were here, but then they followed me around like Dick Tracy. My mom even went in the bathroom with me, which was embarrassing as hell, if you know what I mean, but she didn't care. She started sayin that shit about how she used to change my dirty diapers and she didn't care nothin bout standin there until I got through. And she did. She sat in there while I took my shower, too, and then when we all got ready to go to bed, Daddy got this really sad look on his face, and he put this mutha-fucker right back on me and carried his happy ass to bed like "this shit is hurting me more than it's hurting you." I hate when people say that shit to their kids. That is bullshit. Muthafuckas be whipping their kids ass saying some shit like that. The kid should stop cryin and say, just beat me, okay? Don't beat me and bullshit me, too.

[*Laughs.*] Like I'm gonna say some shit like that to my Dad. I used to try to scream real loud when he would beat me so he'd feel bad and quit. It usually worked. He didn't wanna be whippin me in the first place. I didn't even get my first whippin til I was thirteen. I kept run-nin away from rehab and hangin out and he didn't know what else to do. Me neither, so we lookin at each other like, well? And I'm thinkin, do somethin if you gonna do somethin or leave me alone so I can go get high! So he took off his belt and hit me a couple of times, but it wadn't bad or nothin. My dad don't have the heart for that shit.

See, the shit they don't understand is that I like to be high. I like the way it feels. I was in rehab last time and they was goin around the circle like they always do so you can introduce yourself and con-fess how sorry you are to be a dope fiend and then everybody cry wit you and tell you some shit about yourself they just thought of since they met you ten minutes ago and you suppose to say, "oh, shit" and decide not to smoke no more rock. It's bullshit, so when they got around to me, I said, My name is Rosa Jenkins and I just like to get high! So everybody laughed and started sayin shit like I know that's right! and the counselor got mad at me and told me wadn't nothin funny about bein a dope fiend and I said, that's where you wrong. Everything is funny about being a dope fiend! And that was before my pops had even come up with this chain thing. But I already knew the shit was out. Here lately, I been laughin at the same shit Jesus find funny, and you know what that mean!

The real bullshit of it is when people talk to you about this shit, the part they always leave off is how good it feel when you doin it. Ain't

nobody robbin their grandmother for some shit that don't feel good. That don't make no sense.
    I gotta pee. I can't close the door all the way with this muthafucker on, so don't look!

[*She crosses awkwardly toward the bathroom door. Black.*]

[*Slide up: DAY FOUR*]

[ROSA *is pacing as rapidly as she can with the chain. She is smoking a cigarette. She has mastered walking with it well enough so that her turns now include a practiced flip of the chain that allows her to progress much more efficiently than she did the first few days. The chain is now less a strange imposition and more a constant irritant.*]

ROSA: [*Snubbing out her cigarette in an ashtray that is already overflowing. She continues pacing. Reaches into her pocket and takes out another cigarette. Lights it with a bic lighter, still pacing. Inhales deeply, coughs, snubs this one out too.*] My dad says I should try not to start smokin cause it's bad for my health. [*Laughs.*] Still trippin. [*Lights another cigarette, inhales, makes a face.*] I hate cigarettes, but I gotta smoke something. I am jonesin' like a muthafucka. My mom keeps tellin me to just take it one day at a time and shit like they tell you in rehab. That is bullshit. This is like a minute by minute trip, right? I want to get high so bad … damn! My fingernails wanna get high. My damn toenails wanna get high! "One day at a time." I hate that bullshit.
    Jesus shoulda been lookin for me by now. That muthafucka. He don't give a shit about me. He never did. He just hung around me for the … Shit, I don't know why he hung around me. He don't even know I'm here. I know he don't know I'm here or he woulda figured out some way to contact me. He could slide a note under the door or some shit. [*Sudden thought.*] Damn! If he could slide a letter under … [*She goes to check how wide the space is under the door. She becomes very agitated. She tears a few pages out of a magazine and folds them like a business size letter. She runs this under the door to see how wide a piece of something could be slipped underneath. There is plenty of room.*]
    Goddam! Goddam! [*She paces excitedly.*] He could slip me some shit under there. He could slip me some shit under there every goddam day. They'd never know it. I'll smoke it in the morning and by the time they get home, they won't even be able to smell nothin. Shit!

Why didn't I think of that before? I gotta get word to Jesus. I gotta let him know what he needs to do. [*She looks around for a piece of paper and a pencil and begins to write a letter quickly.*]

[*Slide fade in and hold for 20 seconds while she writes: Dear Jesus, They got me chained in the house. Bring dope. Rosa.*]

[ROSA *looks critically at the letter and makes an alternation. Slide changes to reflect rewritten letter: Dear Jesus, They got me chained in the house. Bring dope. Forever your girl, Rosa.*]

[*Slide fades out.*]

[ROSA *folds the letter and then looks around quickly. It dawns on her that she doesn't have any way to get it to him.*] Shit! [*She drags the chain toward the window, but can't reach it. She tries to tug it toward the telephone. Too short. In frustration, she begins to pull and tug at the chain in a rage.*] Goddam it!

I ... want ... this ... shit ... off ... of ... me!

[*She tears up the letter to Jesus in a rage and sits down, rocking back and forth rapidly.*]

I'm not gonna make it. I'm gonna die up in this muthafucka all by myself. I feel like shit and can't do a damn thing about it. I know where the shit at. I know who got it and how to make em give it up and I can't get a goddam thing. They're killin me. They're killin me. [*A beat, then trying to calm herself.*] But it's gonna be okay. I just gotta hang in there til I'm eighteen, then they got no power over me no more. Jesus say when I get eighteen; I should move in wit him since he got plenty of room. I'm down wit it. I know Jesus dig me and he always got enough rock for us to get high. [*A beat.*] Where is that mutha-fucka? He shoulda come up here and beat on the door and holler or some shit. He could ride up the hall on a big ass white horse like they do in the movies. I would love that shit. I love when somethin weird happens. Somethin you ain't seen two hundred times a day every day. Sometimes I feel like I seen everything they got to show and ain't none of it shit. Ain't none of it shit. [*A beat, then* ROSA *yells several times in loud succession in complete frustration.*] Jesus ain't shit. I ain't shit. Ain't none of it shit. [*Begins to laugh.*] So what the fuck am I cryin about then, right? If ain't none of it shit, who gives a fuck about it? I just wanna get high, you understand? I don't give a fuck one way or the other, I just need to get high. Goddam, I need to get high!

When you start smokin this shit, they don't tell you how bad your ass gonna feel when you ain't got none. They forget to tell you bout that shit, right?

You know the funny shit is, I was almost glad to see my daddy when he came to get me. I hadn't seen Jesus in two days and them niggas was acting crazy as shit. He told them he had the hundred he owed them at the crib and he was gonna leave me there with em while he went to get it so they would know he wadn't bullshittin. He ain't said shit to me about that shit, so I said, say, what? He hadn't even told me about owing nobody when we busted up in there or I wouldn't a gone in the first place. Niggas be slitting people's throat for two dollars and here he come owing some niggas I ain't nevah seen before a hundred dollars. He knew I was pissed, cause he said, don't worry bout that shit, baby: I'll be right back and we'll go over to the house and I'll put the rest of the niggas out and we'll get fucked up, just me and you.

Bullshit, right? But I'm so stupid, I believe the muthafucka. Okay, baby, I say, or some stupid shit like that. I shoulda said, no, muthafucka. You tell me where the shit is, I'll go get it and they can hold you hostage til I get back. But I was tryin to hang, you know? That's where I fucked up. That muthafucka kissed me good-by and shit and walked on out the damn door and I ain't seen the nigga since. At first them niggas had a lot of shit to smoke, so we kept getting high and they didn't say too much to me about nuthin. But then when Jesus didn't show for a long time, they started askin me where he was. Like I knew anything about the shit! I said I didn't know where the nigga was and they said he better bring back a hundred dollars or they gonna fuck me up. I ain't even in the shit, right, but they gonna fuck me up!

So I start figuring what I'm gonna do to get out of the shit and one of em asks me how much would I charge him for some pussy and I say a hundred dollars and he say I must think my pussy made outta gold and "I tell him I can make him get off good by just watchin me cause I'm that good" and he look at the other one and they both laugh and say, maybe the ho do got a pussy made a gold. Show me, say the one who started the shit in the first place and I tell him it gotta be just me and him cause I don't want them to jump me or anything. Niggas get brave when they got they boys watchin. I know I can handle one, but I ain't down wit muthafuckas tryin to run a train and shit. So we went in the bedroom and he closed the door and told me to hit it.

So I pulled my panties to the side like Jesus showed me and started rubbin myself and lookin at his face and he grinned at me and started rubbin hisself through his jeans. I always watch their faces cause that's how you know if they dig it or not. Then he unzip his pants so he can hold his dick in his hand and it was feeling alright to me too, even though Jesus wadn't there to call my name, and I'm thinkin maybe this ain't gonna be so bad after all, but then the nigga reached out and grabbed my hand and tried to make me sit down on his lap while he still got his thing out and shit! And I'm tryin to tell him I ain't down wit it cause a AIDS and shit and he tellin me he ain't no faggot and we sorta wrestlin around and I'm tryin not to make no noise cause I don't want his boy to come in to see what's up, and that's when my dad started beatin on the door and hollerin and shit and all hell broke loose.

They was gettin ready to shoot through the door at first, and I said no, that sound like my dad! So they told him if he didn't pay the hundred dollars I owed them they'd blow my brains out right in front of him. My daddy just stood there for a minute lookin at that nigga holdin his 9 millimeter against my head and I'm thinking, my daddy ain't got that kinda money! I'm dead! And then he reached in his pocket and took out a roll a money and handed it to the nigga who had been in the bedroom with me. The nigga counted it right in front of my daddy and it was a hundred dollars exactly. That's how I know Jesus the one told him to come get me. How else my daddy gonna be walkin around Harlem with a pocketful of cash like he the dope man and shit.

Then that nigga told my daddy to get my little crack addict ass outta his place and pushed me so hard I fell against his chest. My daddy didn't even look at me. He took off his jacket and put it around my shoulders and we walked the three blocks home with him holdin my arm like you do a little kid when they been bad. He wadn't sayin shit. When we got home, my moms was there and she started cryin and holdin my face up so she could look at me and shit. I know I looked like shit. I hadn't eaten in two three days and my clothes were all twisted around from tusslin with that nigga in the bedroom. And I know my hair was all over my head cause she kept smoothin it down and I could feel it risin right back up again and she'd smooth it down again and it would rise on back up. My head was itchin too, but I couldn't scratch or nothin because my mom was huggin me and she had my arms pinned down at my sides and you can't push your momma off you, even if you want

to, so I'm standin there tryin to get her to calm down and I catch a eye-
ful of my pops sittin at the table and tears just runnin down his face.
He ain't cryin or hollerin or nothin. He just sittin there lookin at me
and momma stumblin around the room like we drunk.

That hurt me worse than anything. I never seen my daddy cry
in my life. Never, I seen him mad plenty of times, but not over me.
He be mad about some niggas actin a fool or some crackers fuckin over
him or somethin mama said that didn't sit right, but he never cried.
He didn't cry when his momma died. Took the phone call, drove down
south and buried her, came back and never broke. So I felt real bad
when I saw him cryin over me. I love my daddy ...

So I got away from mama and I went over and stood in front of
him and I said, don't worry about me, daddy. I'm okay. And he just
looked at me and tears runnin all down his chin and he wadn't wipin
shit. Act like he didn't even know he was doin it. I didn't have no
kleenex or nothin, but I hated to see him like that, so I just wiped him
off a little with my sleeve, right? He caught my hand and held it so
hard I thought he was gonna crush my damn fingers and he just
looked at me and started sayin my name over and over and over like
he wasn't sure it was even me: Rosa, Rosa, Rosa! And my mom on the
other side of the room runnin around hollerin and shit.

It was almost like I was somewhere else watchin it. It was too weird
to be happenin to me for real. When I went to bed, I could still hear
my mom in the other room cryin and everytime I woke up, my dad
would be sittin right by my bed, just lookin at me like he in a dream
or somethin. Then one time I got up to go to the bathroom and he
walked right wit me and stood there outside the door and waited for
me and before I got back into bed he hugged me real hard and I could
feel him shakin like he was jonesin worse than me. Scared the shit
outta me. I figured my shit must be even raggedier than I thought if
it making my daddy shake.

It's no way for me to tell him how it feels, you know what I
mean? They don't understand nothin about none of it so there's no
place to start tellin them anything. They shoulda kept their country
asses in Tuskegee, Alabama.

My daddy used to sing when we lived down there. He can sing,
too. He sound like Luther Vandross a little bit. Him and my momma
used to sing in the car. Raggedy ass car they got from somebody. We
drove that muthafucka all the way up here, though. Soon as we got
to Harlem, the muthafucka broke down. I used to ask my pops if the
car had a broke down in Brooklyn, would he a stayed in Brooklyn and

he would laugh and say he probably would.

[*A beat.*]

    I think that nigga was gonna rape me if my daddy hadn't busted up in there. And that wadn't gonna be the worst of it. Jesus wadn't comin back no time soon. That's why he called my pops and told him where I was. [*Laughs.*] He busted up in there, though. My daddy crazy. They coulda blown him away with his Alabama ass. [*A beat.*] I don't think he'd a brought me up here if he'd a known what these niggas up here were like. They treacherous up here in New York. You think you ready for it, but you not ready. These niggas don't care nothin bout you. Jesus spose to be my friend, and look how he act! [*A beat.*] My daddy bad, though. He was beatin on that door like he was packin a Uzi and he didn't have shit. Not even no stick or nothin. He just standin there talkin shit about: Where my baby girl at? Where you got my Rosa?
    And I'm hollerin: Here I am, daddy! Here I am!

[*Black.*]

[*Slide up: DAY FIVE*]

[ROSA *is clicking rapidly through the channels on the small t.v. on the table. It is a tiny black and white model with a very fuzzy picture. She tries in vain to adjust it and find something she likes … Finally snaps it off, frustrated and begins to pace. The chain is still in place, but by now she handles it casually as if it has always been there.*]

    I been tryin to find somethin to overstimulate me. My mom said they real proud of me cause I'm actin like my old self so they gonna let me have t.v. today. How else I'm gonna act chained to the damn radiator? My old self. Who the hell is that? They mean my Alabama self. My before I met Jesus self. My don't know nothin bout crack rock self. That's who they lookin for. [*A beat.*] I miss her too, but I think girlfriend is gone, gone, gone.

[*She paces, but slowly, She's thinking.*]

    My daddy say I been doin so good, he ain't gonna chain me but a couple more days. Just to be sure. I started to tell him, it take longer than that to be sure, but I didn't say nothin. If I say some shit like that, he'll never take this damn chain offa my leg!

He ask me was I worried about the street takin me back if he take the chain offa me. He sound so serious when he say shit like that, but to me, he just be trippin. Like the street some kind of weird, scary shit waitin for you in the alley instead of a bunch of niggas you know tryin to get paid and get high.

But how my gonna tell him that shit? So I told him no. I wasn't worried about the street takin me back. And he hug me and shit and tell me there is nothin out there for me. I say, I know that's right.

[*She tries t.v. again. Turns it off.*]

The thing is, after a couple of days when you don't watch t.v. seem like when you go back to it, ain't nothin on there you wanna see. You gotta let it stay on for a little while without payin no attention, then it start lookin good to you again, otherwise that shit is too lame.

My pops told me I should pray instead of gettin high. No bull-shit. He really did tell me that. I never been to no religious rehab, but I know some people who did. They tell you shit like that all the time. Let God take the place of the drugs in your life. Give it all to God. Shit like that. It works for some muthafuckas, I guess, but I don't believe all that shit. I used to go to church when I was little cause I like to listen to the choir, but I never did get into prayin a whole lot.

I used to like to sneak and look at people while they be prayin with their eyes closed.

They be looking so serious, frownin up and shit. I don't know why people think they gotta look all ugly and shit to talk to God. I figure if the muthafucka — scuse me! — if His Highness is really God and a bad muthafucka, he oughta be able to let you talk just sittin down someplace lookin like you look when you just bein regular. I rather have niggas just talk to me that way than be frowning up and shit, but I ain't God, right? So what the fuck am I talkin about?

I told my dad I wish I believe in God, but I don't. It take time, my dad tell me. You have to get to know him just like any good friend. You have to put the time in to get the goody out. That's what he said. He talkin bout God and shit and then he come talkin bout the goody! He so country sometime!

[*A beat.*]

I been thinkin bout if I wanna keep smokin that shit or not. No, I mean really thinkin about it for myself. It can make you do shit that is really fucked up. I done some fucked up shit myself when I was high, or tryin to get high. I told you I stole my grandmamma's check. I stole lots of people checks. Cash and carry. Old people be lookin all worried cause they check ain't come and I know I smoked that shit up two days ago. And you don't care neither! You just say, fuck it.

Like, I keep thinkin bout how Jesus left me with them niggas I didn't even know! He didn't care what they did to me. They coulda thrown me out the window. And they do that shit, too! Old crack-head niggas threw a girl out the window right around the comer from here just a week ago. Took her clothes off first so when she hit the ground her titties and shit was all out. People standin around laughin and she dead as shit. Nobody even covered her up or nothin.

My daddy told me only God stronger than crack. I tell him this chain been doin a pretty good job. I was just kiddin, but I think it made him feel bad cause his face got all sad and shit. [*A beat.*] I told him I just meant it's hard once you can come and go when you want to not to just go anywhere you can think of goin, right? Even if you not thinkin about it by yourself, somebody gonna remind me to think about smokin that rock. They gonna be goin there, or comin from there or lookin for some money to get there or somethin. It's not like you gotta be lookin for the shit.

[*A beat.*]

He told me he knew I was a good girl and he trusted me. I wanted to say, hey, man! This is goddam Harlem! Trust ain't in it! [*A beat.*] I don't trust nobody. [*A beat.*] Not about no shit like this. It ain't a goddam thing out there but a bunch of niggas gonna die and wanna take me wid em. Ain't a thing out there.

[*She looks around.*]

At least in here, ain't nobody fuckin with me. I got food. I got a bathroom. I even got t.v. and shit, so how bad can it be?

[*Suddenly angry.*]

And what the fuck you lookin at?

[*Black.*]

[*Slide up: DAY SIX*]

[ROSA *sits on the couch, smoking. She is rubbing her ankle distractedly and thinking. She snubs out the cigarette deliberately, still thinking. She gets up and walks across the room. The chain is no longer on her leg, but she is still limping slightly and whenever she is not moving, she rubs her ankle as if it were a little sore.*]

She crosses to the telephone, which is in evidence in the room for the first time, picks it up and dials hesitantly. She hangs up before she finishes the number. Thinks for a minute. Dials again. She waits for it to ring several times.

Who is this? ... Let me speak to Jesus. Rosa. [*Waits for him to come to the phone, when he does, she jumps on him angrily.*] Where you been, muthafucka? Yeah, this is Rosa. Who the fuck you think it was? I know the nigga told you Rosa. You know another Rosa now beside me? Where the fuck you been? ... No! Don't tell me shit! I don't wanna hear it! You left me, muthafucka! They could have fucked me right up and where the fuck were you? ... I said don't tell me shit! ... I don't wanna hear it. They had me chained up because of your triflin ass! ... You heard me! Chained up by the foot like a goddam dog! Right in the living room. If you had brought your ass over here you would have known that shit. ... Don't tell me that shit! You know they be workin all day just like all the other country ass niggas in Harlem. You think they boss give them the week off so they can sit home and watch out for their dope fiend daughter? You know better than that shit, muthafucka. You just didn't give a shit. Got me started smokin that shit and now you just don't give a damn, do you? Well, fuck you, Jesus! Fuck you! ... No, I haven't finished. I got a lot more shit to say to your trifling ass ... [*He interrupts her now until he breaks her rhythm and she begins to be listening more than she is fussing. Her demeanor changes from angryly belligerent to petulant to needy over the course of the conversation.*] No. Nobody ain't told me nothin about where you been. I ain't seen nobody, I told you! I been chained up! ... Where you been? Why? For real? When? They came to your place? Them two you left me wit? ... Then why you leave me wit 'em? ... But if you don't know, you spose to take me wit you and not take a chance, you know? ... They coulda killed me, Jesus! You know I'm not lyin! ... No. ... No ... Nothing like that happened ... I can handle myself,

I been tellin you that. ... I ain't scared of no crackhead niggas. ...
Not even you! ... What you mean how long since I been high? I ain't
doin that shit no more, muthafucka cause I ain't no muthafuckin
dope fiend, alright? I been up here without shit for five days, right?
And I handled it! I am handlin it! So fuck you, Jesus! Fuck you! ... No.
My mom be home in a few minutes so don't bring your black ass up
here. That's right. Not tomorrow either. I don't need that shit. I
just called to let you know not to bring your ass around me and when
you see me on the street, don't even act like you know me, you junkie
muthafucka. ... You ... you
    You left me!

[*Black.*]

[*Slide up: DAY SEVEN*]

[ROSA *is looking out the window. Smoking. She smokes it down to the end,
snubs it out and lights another. She keeps her eyes fixed on the street even
while she is getting another cigarette. She is waiting. She goes to the table.
Sits. She goes to the couch. Sits. She stands near the door and listens. Crosses
to the window. Scans the street. Nothing. She sits again in silence, then
speaks slowly and fiercely to herself.*]

    Fuck this shit, okay? Just fuck it!

[*She snubs out another cigarette. Turns on t.v. Off. Picks up the phone,
starts to dial. Stops. Hangs up. She is very agitated. She sits and sighs
deeply.*]

    Okay, look. This is a prayer, okay? [*A beat.*] I can't do that shit.

[*She is pacing again. She stops suddenly near the closet and slowly reaches
for the knob. She reaches in and gets the bag her dad had the chain in. She
takes it out and goes over to the couch with it. She takes it out, handling it
gingerly. She feels the weight and the chill of it. It is completely familiar
and absolutely mysterious. There is both resignation and comfort in her handling of the chain. She may even place the shackle around her wrist like a
bracelet. She suddenly takes it off of her wrist quickly and puts it down, but
not away. She realizes what she is considering and the thought horrifies her.
She sits looking at the chain for a beat and then reaches toward it again.*]

[*There is a sudden furtive knock at the door. She draws her hand back guiltily. She goes quickly and quietly to the door. She listens. Another furtive knock. She speaks quietly.*]

Jesus? [*A beat.*] Jesus, is that you?

[*She begins to quickly unbolt the locks and chains on the door, fumbling in her anxiousness to get the locks open. When she does, she takes a deep breath, closes her eyes for a minute and then opens the door.*]

[*Black.*]

END OF PLAY

David Dozer

THE MILLING CROWD DIES

David Dozer

David Dozer has written more than 250 plays of various lengths between a minute and an hour long about Charles and Emily Ann Andrews, the young married couple who adopts an old man from the Welfare Department. As "Poisoned Arts," they were produced serially on radio between 1967 and 2000 where they still broadcast live or on recording over WBAI-New York and other Pacifica Network stations. Longer episodes of "Poisoned Arts," including *Poisoned Art Traveling Radio, Last Days of the Planet Arth, On the Sapohanakin Trail, The Giant Cricket* and *Late Night Spots* were also produced for the stage at the Lenox Arts Center, the Manhattan Theatre Club and Cornelia Street Café.

Dozer was born in Pittsburgh where he attended Carnegie Mellon University as a playwriting major in the Drama Department. He was an actor in the improvisational theatre companies The Premise, The Compass Group Banana Game Theatre, The Fourth Wall and The Severn Darden Players. He has appeared in such films as *Bloodbrothers, Hooper, The Telephone Book, Young Doctors in Love* and *Dog Day Afternoon*. He played Corporal/Sgt. Groves in the TV series *M*A*S*H*. In collaboration with Janet Coleman, he has written and performed on stage, film, television, radio and cabaret. Coleman and Dozer's touring production of "*The Coffeehouse Years of Dig Rezod: A Dada Beatnik Cabaret*" was based on Dozer's college poetry and plays. Dozer is also the author of an opera *Dead Leaves, Brief Theatre, Heavy Duty Radio Theatre, People, A Short Horror Comedy* and *Dracula: The Vampire is Not Strictly a Demon*.

SCENE ONE

Onboard a cardboard steamship CHARLES ANDREWS *and* DR. HOLZENCHEESE, *a young man and his psychiatrist, are seated on the poop deck in deck chairs with* EMILY ANN ANDREWS, CHARLES'*s attractive young wife who is perched on a higher deck on a deck rail, while* MR. WABURN, *an old man in a sea captain's hat, stands on the top deck.*

An ANNOUNCER *emerges from below and walks up to the microphone.*

ANNOUNCER: Live from planet Earth it's "Emily Ann & Charles"! Charles Andrews, the news anchor at Cat Radio Cable TV, is relaxing in a deck chair onboard the steamship he made with his bare hands. Charles is chatting with Dr. Holzencheese, the government-authorized psychiatrist. Charles and his pretty young wife Emily Ann — the Queen of Space Jazz and the singing dietician of the dada beatnik Dig Rezod Museum; and, as June Jones, the star of Cat Radio Cable TV's "Fireplaces That Make Your Home Colder" — are under observation by Dr. Holzencheese in connection with their continuing care-giving relationship to Mr. Waburn, the old man they adopted for money from the Welfare Department.

[*The* ANNOUNCER *strikes the microphone exiting with it below.*]

CHARLES: Then last night I dreamt that Mr. Waburn had taken over as captain of my ship and had commenced a bombardment of neighboring islands.

[EMILY ANN *performs gymnastics on the rail.* MR. WABURN *pantomimes ordering rockets to be fired for the launching of missiles.*]

DR. HOLZENCHEESE: You have to develop a sense of humor, Mr. Andrews. You take things too seriously.

[*SFX: ROCKETS FIRING, MISSILES LAUNCHING.*]

[*A* SAILOR *enters carrying a tee shirt.*]

SAILOR: Would anyone like to buy a "Why Are Psychiatrists Crazy?" tee shirt?

[*SFX: DISTANT BOOMS OF EXPLODING MISSILES.*]

CHARLES: Oh, that's funny.

DR. HOLZENCHEESE: No. It is not.

CHARLES: But you told me to develop a sense of humor.

DR. HOLZENCHEESE: Some things are funny. Other things are not. Captain Waburn, have this man flogged and then hang him.

MR. WABURN: I will, Dr. Holzencheese. Just as soon as I complete the bombardment of Bermuda.

[SAILOR *exits.*]

CHARLES: Emily Ann, Dr. Holzencheese wants to execute a sailor just as soon as Mr. Waburn finishes the bombardment of Bermuda.

EMILY ANN: Maybe it's the salt air, Charles, but everything seems hilarious today. Execute a sailor. The bombardment of Bermuda.

[*She laughs. Blackout.*]

SCENE TWO

At Cat Radio Cable TV, on the set of "Fireplaces That Make Your Home Colder," the ANNOUNCER *enters carrying the floor mic. He sets it down.*

ANNOUNCER: On the set of "Fireplaces That Make Your Home Colder" at Cat Radio Cable TV, Charles Andrews, news anchor, is waiting for the rehearsal to end so that before his newscast he can get something to eat with his pretty young wife Emily Ann and Mr. Waburn, the old man they adopted from the Welfare Department.

[*The* ANNOUNCER *exits with the mic as* EMILY ANN *enters.*]

EMILY ANN: Charles.

CHARLES: Oh, hi, Em. Are you ready to go out and get something to eat?

EMILY ANN: Not until you change out of that shirt.

CHARLES: Why? It's a brand new shirt I just put on this morning.

EMILY ANN: It's my shirt, Charles. It's one of the twelve new "Why Are Men Lazy?" tee shirts I bought to wear around the house. So why are you wearing it here at my job?

CHARLES: Because it's brand new, it's clean, you have twelve of them and my shirts were all on the other side of the bedroom.

MR. WABURN: Charles is never so lazy he can't come up with a bunch of excuses.

EMILY ANN: You'll have to change out of that shirt, Charles. The crew feels sexually harassed by it.

CHARLES: I'm sure you're exaggerating, Emily Ann.

CREW: No. She is not. We feel sexually harassed by your shirt.

DR. HOLZENCHEESE: Perhaps if you turn the shirt inside out the problem with the crew can be averted.

MR. WABURN: Good thing you hired a psychiatrist, Emily Ann.

EMILY ANN: Thanks, Mr. Waburn.

DR. HOLZENCHEESE: A psychiatrist is trained to turn things inside out.

CHARLES: I don't want to wear a shirt inside out.

SAILOR: Would anyone like to buy an inoffensive tee shirt? I have over a billion different kinds.

[*Blackout.*]

SCENE THREE

In the reception area at Cat Radio Cable TV CHARLES ANDREWS *can be seen doing his newscast inside a large cardboard TV while* EMILY ANN *and* MR. WABURN *sit and wait. The* ANNOUNCER *enters carrying the floor mic. He sets it down.*

ANNOUNCER: While Cat Radio Cable TV newsman Charles Andrews is on a commercial break on his Cat Radio Cable TV newscast, his pretty young wife Emily Ann has a chance to get the opinion of Mr. Waburn, the old man they adopted from the Welfare Department.

[*The* ANNOUNCER *strikes the mic and exits.*]

EMILY ANN: Mr. Waburn, did you hear me sing today's luncheon special at the dada beatnik Dig Rezod Museum?

MR. WABURN: Not yet. Let me hear it, singing dietician.

CHARLES: [*TV.*] Time now for Reporters' Hexagonal Table. Gripe of the day, Liz Korzer, News-Moon Magazine:

LIZ: [*TV.*] A government that tries to help people instead of killing them. Society is in pain and has a right to die.

CHARLES: [*TV.*] Gripe of the day, Dr. Timothy Thunder, Time Date and Destiny Tribune:

TIM: [*TV.*] Pessimism is the problem. And I do not think we will ever get rid of it.

CHARLES: [*TV.*] [*To camera.*] If *you* want to get rid of *your* pessimism you might want to enroll in one of the fine schools of announcing associated with the League of Announcing Schools.

[*Music up and Lights out inside the cardboard TV.*]

[*Blackout.*]

SCENE FOUR

CHARLES, EMILY ANN *and* MR. WABURN *are onboard a cardboard bus.*

EMILY ANN: Charles.

CHARLES: What, Emily Ann?

EMILY ANN: Why have you finally agreed, after all these years of refusing, to go to the theatre?

CHARLES: Oh, I don't know.

> [*The cardboard bus comes to a stop and* CHARLES, EMILY ANN *and* MR. WABURN *get off outside a cardboard theater.*]

This is the theater.

[*A milling* CROWD *oozes onstage.*]

MR. WABURN: Complete with a Goddamned milling crowd out front.

CHARLES: I don't like the looks of this milling crowd.

EMILY ANN: I interviewed this milling crowd on "Fireplaces That Make Your Home Colder."

CHARLES: I hate a crowd that thinks it's famous.

MR. WABURN: "What's next for the Goddamned milling crowd?"

> [EMILY ANN *and* MR. WABURN *follow* CHARLES *as he goes around to the back of the cardboard theater where* DR. HOLZENCHEESE *appears.*]

DR. HOLZENCHEESE: Welcome to "The Evil Sister."

EMILY ANN: Dr. Holzencheese! What a surprise.

CHARLES: Dr. Holzencheese invited me here.

EMILY ANN: You go to the theatre when your government-authorized psychiatrist invites you.

DR. HOLZENCHEESE: It was actually a subpoena.

EMILY ANN: Court ordered culture?

DR. HOLZENCHEESE: Your tax dollars at work.

CHARLES: When does it begin, Dr. Holzencheese?

DR. HOLZENCHEESE: It's already begun.

EMILY ANN: It began already?

DR. HOLZENCHEESE: With the milling crowd.

CHARLES: Emily Ann had the milling crowd on "Fireplaces That Make Your Home Colder."

DR. HOLZENCHEESE: That was before they were given an experimental disease.

EMILY ANN: The milling crowd was given an experimental disease?

DR. HOLZENCHEESE: Another government-sponsored experiment. They are trying to design a disease that will only prove fatal to troublemakers.

CHARLES: I love scientific research.

DR. HOLZENCHEESE: Please take your seats for "The Evil Sister."

[CHARLES, EMILY ANN *and* MR. WABURN *climb into their bleacher seats front and center and* DR. HOLZENCHEESE *strikes a pose.*]

CHARLES: These are great seats.

EMILY ANN: And you love the theatre so much they have to subpoena you to get you here.

[*SFX: CYMBAL CRASH.*]

[*Lights up on* DR. HOLZENCHEESE.]

DR. HOLZENCHEESE: Good evening, lunatics and loved ones. Please make paper airplanes of your subpoenas and launch them toward the stage.

[CHARLES *and others in the* CROWD *make paper airplanes and launch them toward the stage.*]

EMILY ANN: Why didn't I get a subpoena?

DR. HOLZENCHEESE: Act One, Scene One of "The Evil Sister."

[*Musical flourish.* FATHER *and* MOTHER *appear.*]

FATHER: Good morning, Mother.

MOTHER: Good morning, Father.

FATHER: Where is our good son this good morning, Mother.

MOTHER: Here is our good son now.

[SON *enters.*]

SON: Good morning, Mother and Father.

FATHER: Good morning, good son.

MOTHER: Morning is good when the son is a good son.

FATHER: A good son and a good morning are all that any family would ever need.

SON: Everything is good and wonderful.

MOTHER: But what?

SON: Wouldn't it be fun if I had an evil sister?

FATHER: An evil sister?

MOTHER: An evil sister?

SON: I thought it might be fun to have an evil sister.

FATHER: Wouldn't that mean that your mother and I would have an evil daughter?

SON: I never thought of that.

MOTHER: If you want an evil sister we would be more than willing to have an evil daughter. Wouldn't we, father?

FATHER: Of course we would, mother. Anything for our good son.

SON: I'm glad to hear it. I put an ad in the paper for an evil sister.

MOTHER: A want ad for an evil sister?

SON: We can expect a knock at the door at any time.

FATHER: You expect to hire an evil sister?

SON: Her payment would be living here.

MOTHER: That's the payment *I* get.

[*SFX: KNOCK ON THE DOOR.*]

SON: I'll answer the door.

[*SFX: DOOR OPENING.*]

[ROSCO *appears.*]

ROSCO: I'm here in answer to an ad for an evil cousin that I saw in the newspaper.

SON: You are a stupid moron.

ROSCO: Is that part of the job of being the evil cousin?

SON: You have gone to the address of someone advertising for an evil sister, which you've mixed up with the address of someone advertising for an evil cousin.

DR. HOLZENCHEESE: And thus ends Act One, Scene One of "The Evil Sister."

[*SFX: APPLAUSE.*]

[*Lights out on the players onstage. Lights up on the bleachers where audience members are applauding.*]

EMILY ANN: You can tell it's real theatre when there is something about a mix up.

CHARLES: I don't see what's to be learned from a character who is a stupid moron.

MR. WABURN: It's Goddamned obvious.

DR. HOLZENCHEESE: Now Act One, Scene Two of "The Evil Sister" finds the mother, the father and the good son awaiting the next knock on the door that they hope will be an applicant for the job of evil sister.

[*SFX: DOOR KNOCKING.*]

MOTHER: Someone is at the door.

SON: I'll get it.

FATHER: I hope it's an evil sister applicant.

[*SFX: DOOR OPENING.*]

[*A young woman,* RUTH, *appears.*]

RUTH: Is this the address of the people advertising for an evil cousin?

SON: What is wrong with you evil cousin applicants?

RUTH: I am not an evil cousin applicant. I went to the address of the people advertising for an evil cousin by mistake. I'm looking for a job as an evil sister. I'm trying to make sure that this is the right address.

SON: The right address for what?

RUTH: Evil sister.

SON: Yes. Come in.

[*SFX: DOOR CLOSING.*]

RUTH: This room should be completely redecorated.

SON: These would be your parents.

MOTHER & FATHER: Hello.

RUTH: Is this an evil daughter job too?

SON: If you qualify.

RUTH: Qualify? Your mother and father already like me more than they like you.

FATHER: She's right, son.

MOTHER: I was nothing without a daughter.

SON: I get to decide. I ran the ad for the evil sister.

FATHER: She's perfect.

MOTHER: Just what I always wanted.

SON: What is your previous work experience?

MOTHER: Don't pick on your sister.

FATHER: Some day she might marry a rich man and you can visit their yacht.

RUTH: On my previous job I was a harlot.

SON: A harlot?

RUTH: I've had a wide variety of jobs.

SON: Such as.

RUTH: I've been a whore, a slut, nymphomaniac, bimbo and I once was a hooker.

[*Musical crescendo.* SON *exits.*]

DR. HOLZENCHEESE: Act Two, Scene Two is one year later.

RUTH: Mom and Dad, do me a favor.

FATHER: Anything.

MOTHER: What, dear?

RUTH: When you die, could you both be cremated and buried in the same grave so I can have the other one?

FATHER: You want the other grave?

RUTH: So that I can be buried next to you.

FATHER: That is so sweet.

MOTHER: Of course, dear.

FATHER: Where is that semi-good son we had around here? I want to make sure he knows about these burial arrangements.

RUTH: Your son is dead.

FATHER: Oh?

MOTHER: When did he die?

RUTH: Almost a year ago.

FATHER: It's funny we never noticed, isn't it, mother?

RUTH: Mother is dead.

FATHER: Then it's just you and me.

RUTH: Not for long.

FATHER: Now I'm dead.

RUTH: I'm talking to a ghost.

MOTHER: I want to be a ghost too.

RUTH: Go right ahead. Who cares? You're both dead.

SON: Then I shall return as a ghost too.

FATHER: Son.

MOTHER: Your evil sister has caused us all to die.

SON: To tell you the truth, I'm sorry I ran that ad in the newspaper for an evil sister.

[*Lights out on the players onstage.*]

[*SFX: APPLAUSE.*]

[*Lights up on the bleachers where* CHARLES, EMILY ANN *and* MR. WABURN *are applauding.*]

DR. HOLZENCHEESE: And thus ends our play. Sorry to announce that the milling crowd that you saw at the beginning have all died. While providing valuable information to the government about dealing with troublemakers, the Dr. Holzencheese Theatre is pleased to provide you with another great tragedy.

CHARLES: That was a great tragedy.

MR. WABURN: Goddamned obvious.

EMILY ANN: To me it was a great tragedy that was also a great comedy.

MR. WABURN: And it's not just that a group of troublemakers die that makes it a comedy.

EMILY ANN: No. It's that a group of troublemakers die simultaneously.

CHARLES: Everything the government does makes me laugh.

EMILY ANN: But why did Dr. Holzencheese insist that you see this play, Charles? What is the relevance?

CHARLES: I don't know, Emily Ann. How funny the government is? I know Dr. Holzencheese wants me to laugh.

MR. WABURN: It's Goddamned obvious.

EMILY ANN: It is, Mr. Waburn?

MR. WABURN: This play sends a Goddamned clear message to one Charles Andrews: that it's better to adopt a cranky old man from the Welfare Department, than it is to hire an evil sister out of the newspaper.

CHARLES: I'd say it's a toss up.

[CHARLES, EMILY ANN *and* MR. WABURN *continue to sit with the dead* MILLING CROWD *seated around them. Blackout.*]

THE END

Rich Orloff

PRAGUE SUMMER

Rich Orloff

Rich Orloff has had three other one-act comedies included in the *Best American Short Play* series: *The Whole Shebang [1994-1995]*, *I Didn't Know You Could Cook [1996-1997]*, and *Oedi [19978-1998]*. His full-length plays include the comedies *Damaged* Goods [winner, *1994* Playwrights First Award], *Veronica's Position* [winner, *1995* Festival of Emerging American Theatre], *Big Boys* [winner, *1997* InterPlay International Play Festival], *Someone's Knocking* [critic's pick, *Back Stage West, 1998*], *Domestic Tranquility* [winner, *1999* Theatre Conspiracy New Play Contest], and Guy *Stuff* [finalist, 2000 Santa Fe Performing Arts Competition], and the drama *Shedding Light* [winner, 2000 Abeles Foundation Playwrights Award]. His comic revue Oy! was produced off-Broadway, and his play *Vietnam 101: The War on Campus,* based on true stories of campus life during the Vietnam era, has been done at colleges across the country.

Rich has taught playwriting at his alma mater Oberlin College, at City Theater in Miami, and for the Connecticut Young Playwrights program. Rich has also written for newspapers, magazines, television, radio, industrial films, and educational videos. He is a regular contributor to *The Dramatist* magazine and is a member of the Dramatists Guild.

CHARACTERS

LADISLAV: *a Czech born in the late 1940's.*
XAVIER: *a Czech born in the late 1940's.*
ZELDA: *an American in her early thirties.*

PLACE: *An outdoor cafe in Prague, the Czech Republic.*

TIME: *The early 1990's. Late one summer afternoon.*

LADISLAV *sits at a table in an outdoor cafe in Prague. We hear the sounds of people chatting and silverware clinking on a warm summer day.* LADISLAV *sips a cup of coffee and reads. He is dressed in the manner of someone who hasn't much money and who, if he did, wouldn't spend it on clothes.*
    LADISLAV *puts the book down and stares up at something high.* XAVIER *enters and, after a moment, recognizes* LADISLAV. XAVIER *wears a stylish suit and carries a briefcase.*

XAVIER: Ladislav?

LADISLAV: Xavier!

XAVIER: Sorry I'm late.

LADISLAV: That's okay.

XAVIER: You know how business is.

LADISLAV: I've heard rumors.

XAVIER: [*Glad to see him.*] Ladislav, after all these years. Is it truly you?

LADISLAV: That is such a daunting question on so many levels, I can only reply, I believe I believe I am.

XAVIER: That is the kind of answer nobody but Ladislav could give.

LADISLAV: Well, if everybody else is eliminated, then I'm even more confident that I'm me.

XAVIER: Ladislav!

LADISLAV: Xavier! You look good.

XAVIER: Thank you. You know what I always said about appearances.

LADISLAV: "They're all you need."

XAVIER: I'm so glad you agreed to meet me. You know, I had several of my associates search all over Prague for you.

LADISLAV: You're kidding.

XAVIER: And to think you work just across the street from my café.

LADISLAV: So you own this café now?

XAVIER: Well, I recently gained an interest in it.

LADISLAV: I hear you've gained an interest in everything profitable in Prague.

XAVIER: And much that isn't profitable, too.

LADISLAV: From what I've read —

XAVIER: So tell me: What are you up to these days?

LADISLAV: Observation, reflection and rumination.

XAVIER: You haven't changed.

LADISLAV: Change is inevitable. Even the effort to not change changes one. Thus, philosophically I disagree with you 100%. Other than that, I think you're right.

XAVIER: How many years has it been?

LADISLAV: Let's see; it's 1992. Over twenty years, I think.

XAVIER: [*Pointing across the street.*] And how did you end up working there?

LADISLAV: Usually I take the bus.

XAVIER: Ladislav, I – A man of your intelligence working as a, a ticket seller to an observation deck.

LADISLAV: People say the tower on the east side of the Charles Bridge offers the best view of Prague.

XAVIER: But –

LADISLAV: You can almost see its potential.

XAVIER: How long have you been doing this?

LADISLAV: Eighteen years.

XAVIER: Eighteen years?! Is this the best job you could find?

LADISLAV: It depends on how you define "best". It was not best in my parents' eyes or my friends' eyes, and I doubt you would define it as "best", and yet when I was in my twenties and I considered the jobs the Party would let me have, I knew that this was the job in which I would face the fewest moral paradoxes. Also, during all those years when tourism was limited to East Germans, Poles and the few Westerners who could get visas, I could get a great deal of uninterrupted reading done. Of course, now that Prague's become the tourist mecca of Eastern Europe, I read very little.

XAVIER: Ladislav, something's not right about this.

LADISLAV: I agree. They should allow fewer tourists.

XAVIER: No, I mean, a man of your intellect and vision. You should be, you should be working for me!

LADISLAV: And what skills of mine could be useful to you?

XAVIER: Observation, reflection and rumination.

LADISLAV: But you're a businessman. How could that ——

XAVIER: Ladislav, when we planned demonstrations together in the late sixties, nobody was as good as you at developing ideas that inspired hope in a better tomorrow. You took ideas and made them fly. Why don't you do that for me?

LADISLAV: Do what for you?

XAVIER: Think about the future for me, about how the Czech Republic can compete and prosper in a new world.

LADISLAV: I think I'll stay with my job at the tower.

XAVIER: Ladislav, I need you.

LADISLAV: I'm sure you can ——

XAVIER: Do you know how many boring thinkers there are out there? I haven't found anyone who could make ideas soar like you could.

LADISLAV: That was a long time ago.

XAVIER: I pay very well.

LADISLAV: I earn enough.

XAVIER: If you worked for me, you wouldn't be so depressed.

LADISLAV: I like depression. It feels honest.

XAVIER: You romanticize depression, and you always did.

LADISLAV: And you romanticize business.

XAVIER: Ladislav.

LADISLAV: Look, you're happy where you are, and I'm miserable where I am. Why can't we leave it at that?

XAVIER: Because leaving things as they are offends my entrepreneurial spirit.

LADISLAV: Xavier, enough. All anyone in this country talks about anymore is business.

XAVIER: What's wrong with that?

LADISLAV: Whatever happened to philosophy? Remember when you and I would stay up till dawn having heated debates over which was better, to turn into a cockroach or a rhinoceros?

XAVIER: [*Dismissive.*] We were college students.

LADISLAV: We had ideals.

XAVIER: Ideals were all we could afford.

LADISLAV: Xavier —

XAVIER: It's time to get out of your tower, Ladislav. Like it or not, the future belongs to those who are willing to think, work and risk in a market economy.

LADISLAV: Xavier, the future you describe is like a woman dressed in tight clothes and sexy makeup. Attractive, yes, but unlikely to satisfy my deeper longings. She offers excitement without meaning.

XAVIER: I've gone out with that woman you described, and I found meaning in her.

LADISLAV: I believe you. And I hope you don't consider this an insult, but I envy your capacity for superficial happiness.

XAVIER: Well, if I can't change your thinking, I'm expecting a friend who I know can.

LADISLAV: And what type of friend is this?

XAVIER: One who looks good in tight clothing and sexy make-up.

LADISLAV: How meaningful.

XAVIER: She's an investment banker for a group in the U.S.

LADISLAV: So your relationship with her is business.

XAVIER: Well, let's just say as she's helped me vertically integrate my companies we've also horizontally integrated our relationship.

LADISLAV: Same ol' Xavier. Of all the ideals you sold in 1968, you sold none better than sexual freedom.

XAVIER: That *was* one of my more notable skills, but I confess this woman has captured my heart.

LADISLAV: You're kidding.

XAVIER: Wait till you meet her. She's not only as beautiful as a Porsche and as smart as a Pentium chip, but, well, if I can ever learn to think and act like her, I know I'll always have a place in Prague's future. [*Seeing her approach.*] Ah, here she comes ... Zelda, over here!

[ZELDA *enters. Her appearance is striking not only because she's confident and dynamic, but also because she has two long feelers protruding from her head and six slender legs extending from her soft brown body. All in all, she resembles a cockroach.*]

ZELDA: Hi, hi!

[ZELDA *and* XAVIER *kiss briefly.*]

The meeting exceeded our expectations.

XAVIER: Wonderful. Zelda, *this* is Ladislav Smolak. Ladislav, this is Zelda Fleming.

LADISLAV: Pleased to meet you.

ZELDA: Xavier has told me so much about you.

LADISLAV: He speaks well of you, too.

ZELDA: Does he?

LADISLAV: Xavier has said such wonderful things about you I began to think you descended from heaven.

ZELDA: Really? He treats me like I just crawled out of the woodwork.

XAVIER: So what happened? Did your partners agree to take an interest in me?

ZELDA: Xavier, we want to infest your company with our capital.

XAVIER: Great.

ZELDA: Of course, they want me to be your vice president.

XAVIER: I'm not sure I can afford you.

ZELDA: Don't worry. I work for crumbs.

XAVIER: This is so exciting! We must go out and celebrate.

ZELDA: Fine with me.

XAVIER: Join us, Ladislav?

LADISLAV: I don't think I'd be good company.

ZELDA: [*To* XAVIER.] Have you convinced Ladislav to join the organization?

XAVIER: It seems Ladislav is not interested in capitalism.

ZELDA: I hate to break this to you, Ladislav, but Communism is dead.

LADISLAV: Who said those must be the only two choices?

ZELDA: Is there a third?

LADISLAV: There was once.

ZELDA: When?

LADISLAV: In 1968.

ZELDA: Oh, that.

LADISLAV: Yes, that. Socialism with a human face, a belief in a society in which everyone could flourish, including the capitalistically impaired.

ZELDA: How quaint.

LADISLAV: It inspired a whole country.

ZELDA: For a short time.

LADISLAV: We were invaded by the Soviets.

ZELDA: Still —

LADISLAV: Now we're invaded by McDonald's and Benetton's and the Gap.

XAVIER: And the masses welcome the invaders.

LADISLAV: And what about that better world we once believed in?

XAVIER: That future is past. That was Prague Spring; this is Prague Summer.

ZELDA: We must all change with the times.

LADISLAV: As soon as there's a time I like, I'll change with it.

ZELDA: And what do you plan to do until then, hide in a hole like a mole?

LADISLAV: No. My dream has always been to fly in the sky like a bird.

XAVIER: And where would you fly to?

LADISLAV: To a land where people want to serve society more than they want to serve themselves. To a place where dreams have beautiful shapes without bottom lines.

ZELDA: You know, I was once like you.

LADISLAV: I doubt that.

ZELDA: When I started business school, I was a mouse. I was timid and small, with a stringy little tail.

XAVIER: I can't imagine you like that.

ZELDA: Unfortunately, I could, and so I lived down to my imagination.

XAVIER: How did you ever –

ZELDA: There I was, trapped inside my mousy exterior, getting nowhere, scurrying about in fear, and one day, one day I just realized I had to take a leap of faith to become something better. So I did. A leap of faith. And now here I am, successful and adaptable. Inspiring story, isn't it?

LADISLAV: I will remember it, I assure you.

ZELDA: You don't like me, do you?

XAVIER: Zelda, please.

LADISLAV: It's okay. No, I don't dislike you. But I have no desire to be like you.

ZELDA: No, I could tell from the moment our eyes met. Some folks take one look at me and think "disease carrier". It's jealousy. Let's go, Xavier.

XAVIER: Zelda —

LADISLAV: No, I'll go.

XAVIER: Ladislav, wait. You and I were good friends once.

LADISLAV: I know. I admired you so much. You had such creativity and passion. Nobody could publicize a secret meeting better than you.

XAVIER: My door will always be open to you.

LADISLAV: I'm just afraid it will shut behind me. Goodbye, Xavier. Goodbye, Ms. Fleming. It was most educational meeting you.

ZELDA: And what did you learn?

LADISLAV: I learned the future of the Czech Republic probably does belong to creatures like you. But creatures like me, we're not mice. We're dinosaurs. Goodbye. [LADISLAV exits.]

ZELDA: What a loser.

XAVIER: He's an idealist.

ZELDA: When a less than perfect person is incapable of adapting to a less than perfect world, I don't think it's the world's fault.

XAVIER: I wish I could help him.

ZELDA: If you did, he'd spit on you.

XAVIER: I wouldn't mind.

ZELDA: So my partners want us to begin taking you over immediately.

XAVIER: Just tell me what you want.

ZELDA: Can you put out feelers?

XAVIER: Of course; I'm an entrepreneur.

ZELDA: We also need you to grow four more legs.

XAVIER: Consider it done.

ZELDA: And after that, well, we have such great plans for you. I can't tell you how much I'm looking forward to us merging in every way. When I think of what we'll produce together —

[*During the above speech, the background sounds of the restaurant have increased significantly. People are talking loudly about something.*]

What is all the commotion?

XAVIER: People seem to be staring at the top of the tower.

ZELDA: I wish my eyes were better.

XAVIER: Oh my God!

ZELDA: What?

XAVIER: Ladislav!

ZELDA: What?

XAVIER: Ladislav has climbed over the guard rail onto the edge of the tower!

ZELDA: Why?

XAVIER: There's only one reason anybody ever climbs onto the edge of that tower.

ZELDA: Idiot.

XAVIER: Ladislav!!

ZELDA: I'm sure he can't hear you.

XAVIER: What have we done?

ZELDA: We spoke honestly.

XAVIER: I must get to him.

ZELDA: You'll never get to him.

XAVIER: I just can't stand here and —

[*Suddenly, there's a gasp from the crowd.* LADISLAV *has leapt from the tower.* XAVIER *and* ZELDA *move their heads as they watch him fall and fall. Then, another, lighter gasp comes from the crowd, as* XAVIER *and* ZELDA *move their heads to the side and up.*]

What beautiful wings he grew.

[XAVIER *and* ZELDA *watch* LADISLAV *fly off into the distance.*]

THE END

Jacquelyn Reingold

JOE AND STEW'S THEATRE OF BROTHERLY LOVE AND FINANCIAL SUCCESS

Jacquelyn Reingold

Jacquelyn Reingold's plays, *Girl Gone, Acapulco, String Fever, Dear Kenneth Blake, Dottie and Richie, Tunnel of Love, Jiley & Lednerg, A.M.L.,* and *Freeze Tag,* have been seen at the MCC Theatre, Ensemble Studio Theatre, Naked Angels, HB Playwrights, The Drama League, All Seasons, Atlantic Theatre, ASK Theatre Projects, Shadow Box, Working Theatre; and in London and Australia. Her awards include New Dramatists' 2000 Joe Callaway Award, a commission from EST/Sloan Foundation, New Dramatists' Whitfield Cook, the Kennedy Center's Fund for New American Plays' Roger Stevens Award, two Drama-Logue Awards, a finalist for the Susan Smith Blackburn Prize, and the Greenwall Foundation's Oscar Ruebhausen Award.

Jacquelyn's work has been published in *Best American Short Plays 1997-98, 1996-97,* and *1994-95, Women Playwrights: The Best Plays of 1994, New Dramatists: Best Plays of the Graduating Class 2000,* and by Dramatists Play Service and Samuel French. Her screenplay adaptation of *Girl Gone* has been optioned by Beech Hill Films, and she has written for MTV's *Daria.* She is a recent alum of New Dramatists, and a member of Ensemble Studio Theatre and the HB Playwrights Unit.

Joe and Stew's Theatre of Brotherly Love and Financial Success was originally written for Primary Stages, where a reading was directed by Seth Gordon. It then had many readings at many theatres done by many actors. It was fully staged and produced by All Seasons Theatre, John McCormack, Artistic Director, in January, 2000, directed by Warren Leight, and acted by Ean Sheehy and Greg Esposito. My heartfelt thanks to everyone.

CHARACTERS

STEW: *A cockroach. Smart and sensitive.*
JOE: *His brother. Also a cockroach. Not so smart and not so sensitive.*
THE CRITIC: *A human. Sort of. Off-stage.*

PLACE: *An off-off Broadway theatre.*

TIME: *Any minute.*

NOTE: *Theatre and play references should be adapted/updated to fit place and time where the play is performed.*

The sound of a loud explosion. Lights up. Debris is everywhere. We hear voices from under a pile.

STEW: Whoa! What was that?

JOE: I don't know.

STEW: You ok? Joe?

JOE: I don't know. You?

STEW: I don't know. Where are you?

JOE: I don't know.

STEW: Can you see?

JOE: Not really.

STEW: Me either. That was pretty bright.

JOE: Yeah.

STEW: And loud.

JOE: No kidding.

STEW: That wasn't in last night. Must be new, huh?

JOE: I guess.

STEW: I don't see how it makes sense.

JOE: Didn't make no sense to me.

STEW: I mean dramatically, you know.

[STEW *emerges from the pile. He is a cockroach. He looks around at the mess.*]

STEW: Wow. [*To himself.*] Very realistic. Very site specific. Very breaking the fourth wall.

JOE: What?

STEW: Nothing.

JOE: Ow! Damn.

STEW: You ok?

JOE: Yo, I don't know, I'm stuck. I'm under a beam or somethin'.

STEW: Ok, I'm coming, I'm coming. Just keep talking.

JOE: Three of my damn legs are stuck under a damn two by four and it's cutting off my Goddamn circulation!

[STEW *removes a broomstick [toothpick] from* JOE's *legs. He emerges. He is a cockroach, too.*]

JOE: What was that thing?

STEW: Toothpick. You ok?

JOE: Yeah. I think so.

STEW: Antenna?

JOE: [*He checks.*] Fine.

STEW: Legs?

JOE: All there.

STEW: Carapace?

JOE: In one piece.

STEW: That was close.

JOE: Sure was. Hey, you saved my life, Stew.

STEW: Ah, what are brothers for?

  [*They clap each other on the back.*]

JOE: [*Notices the surroundings.*] Wow. What a mess.

STEW: Impressive, huh?

JOE: Uh oh.

STEW: What?

JOE: Where are those brownie crumbs?! I worked all week to collect them.
  [*He searches.*]

STEW: Uh oh.

JOE: What?

STEW: What do you hear?

JOE: Nothing.

STEW: This is the part in Act 2 where they yell and have that big fight. "You son of a bitch!" "You daughter of a bitch!" Remember?

JOE: Not really.

STEW: We better go look.

JOE: I'll stay here.

[*They look at the audience.*]

STEW: The actors — they're — gone.

JOE: Human toast.

STEW: The audience.

JOE: Burnt to a crisp.

CRITIC: [*Off.*] [*He moans.*] Uuuuhhhh.

JOE: Except for that one.

STEW: The critic.

JOE: He's in pain, but he's alive. What should we do?

STEW: Let him suffer.

JOE: Something happened, huh?

STEW: Joe, remember the bedtime story Grandpa used to tell us about the humans and the atomic bomb and how we'd be only ones to survive?

JOE: Uh, no.

STEW: We'd have cookies and milk while he told us?

JOE: Oh, yeah.

STEW: I guess it's true.

JOE: You mean — ?

STEW: Kaboom.

JOE: You mean?

STEW: The end of the human race.

JOE: You mean?

STEW: The end of all the races.

JOE: You mean?

STEW: Except for us.

JOE: You mean?

STEW: The world is ours.

JOE: You mean there won't be an intermission?

STEW: I guess not.

JOE: I wonder what happened to all those snacks.

STEW: How can you think of that right now?

JOE: What-we gotta eat, right?

STEW: Yeah. I guess.

JOE: [*Singing and dancing.*] *This Land is My Land. This Land is My Land. This Land is My Land. This Land is My Land.*

STEW: What are you so happy about? Except for the suffering and ultimate slow death of the critic, I don't see the cause the for joy.

CRITIC: [*Off.*][*Moans.*] Ouuuugggg.

JOE: No more humans, right?

STEW: Right.

JOE: That means no more Raid, right?

STEW: Right.

JOE: And no more Combat trays.

STEW: Right.

JOE: No more boric acid mixed with sugar.

STEW: Right.

JOE: No more run for your life here comes a big pair of shoes, right?!

STEW: Right.

JOE: Well, *shouldn't* we celebrate? I mean we've taken over the world, right?!!

STEW: Right.

JOE: Isn't that what we always wanted? Stew, *Stew.* Bye bye non profit, hello big bucks! Right? Think of the opportunities. Think of the population explosion. It's unbelievable. We could turn this place into

— into the world's first real roach motel. "Where roaches check in, and then they check out."

STEW: Joe.

JOE: Stew.

STEW: You're not thinking of —

JOE: What?

STEW: Not having a theatre?

JOE: Sure I am.

STEW: I'm speechless.

JOE: That's fine.

STEW: Now wait one second, this is a theatre.

JOE: No, this was a theatre.

STEW: Joe.

JOE: Stew.

STEW: I have something to tell you.

JOE: Yeah?

STEW: I never told this to anyone before.

JOE: Yeah?

STEW: But now seems like a good time. With what's happened.

JOE: Yeah?

STEW: I know we're brothers and all, but I'm well, different.

JOE: You mean — ?

STEW: I'm not like the rest of the family, or even the rest of the species.

JOE: You're not?

STEW: I'm a —

JOE: What?

STEW: A —

JOE: What?

STEW: A —

JOE: *What?*

STEW: A not for profit theatre lover.

JOE: What?

STEW: I love this theatre. That's why we've stayed here for so long.

JOE: I thought it was for the brownies and the chocolate chip cookies, and how they didn't have the money to pay someone to clean up the crumbs.

STEW: No. It's the smell of the green room and the roar of the dressing room, the dust on the pile of scripts in the literary office, the broken air conditioning, the young hopeful faces of the interns, the tears of the playwrights —

JOE AND STEW: — Especially the ones who get produced.

STEW: The constant begging and demeaning of oneself to raise money, the tyranny of the artistic director — how everyone hates him and kisses his ass at the same time — and of course the rehearsals, the performances, the production meetings, the cast parties.

JOE: At least those are good. Lots of hummus.

STEW: The opening night fundraiser for the board.

JOE: Cheese cubes.

STEW: The only thing I hate, of course, is the critic.

CRITIC: [*Off.*][*Moans.*]

JOE: I like the critic, he never picks up his candy wrappers.

STEW: I was born in a trunk.

JOE: You were?

STEW: Well, metaphorically. Actually, we were born behind the refrigerator in the artistic director's fabulously tiny deliciously filthy studio apartment. And on the same day that he murdered our mother and father, he unwittingly gave us a new home by carrying us here in his knapsack.

JOE: Things were different then.

STEW: Yes. The plays were daring, the audience was packed, the tickets were cheap, and the critics were so confused by the enthusiasm, they were kind.

JOE: And now we gotta change with the times. Right? No point in the living in the past. I always wanted to be an entrepreneur. Go into real estate. We could form a partnership. I got lots of ideas. Health clubs, cruise ships, coffee bars. They'll all be dark, damp, and filled with food.

STEW: Joe.

JOE: Stew.

STEW: Haven't you been listening?

JOE: Yeah, haven't you? I mean how many people were in the audience tonight?

STEW: Four. The director, the playwright, the artistic director, the playwright's mother.

JOE: That's not an audience. That's a car pool.

CRITIC: [*Off.*] [*Moans.*]

STEW: And the critic. Five. But I guess he doesn't count. You said humans.

JOE: Look, how big was their debt?

STEW: Big.

JOE: How many fights did they have amongst themselves?

STEW: Many.

JOE: How often were they the butt of jokes in their community?

STEW: Often.

JOE: How badly did the actors try to quit the shows by looking for jobs in the movies?

STEW: Badly.

JOE: Well?

STEW: Well, how bout all the work they've done. That production of *Metamorphosis*? I cried every night.

JOE: I don't remember.

STEW: They served tea with honey in the second act.

JOE: Oh, yeah.

STEW: Think of their dedication to non-commercialism and multiculturalism. The work they did with the disabled, the untalented, the criminally insane. Their commitment in the face of constant failure.

JOE: Stew, this place was a bomb way before the one that dropped in here tonight. I may not be a genius, but I know what I know, and this is not the time and place for a theatre. All you had to do was look at- or crawl over the face of the guy who ran the place. Heart broken and bitter.

STEW: He dedicated his life to this.

JOE: Exactly. And we survived, and he didn't. Whatever they gave us we lived through it: poison, sterilization, DDT, you name it, we beat it; not by jerking each other off in the name of the theatre. This place? On the evolutionary scale, it thrived for maybe a second. Less.

STEW: But that's why we'd do better.

JOE: Stew, we're talking survival of the fittest, not survival of the artistic! The answer is: No Way.

[STEW *starts to sob.*]

Oh, geez, don't cry. Look, uh maybe a movie theatre, ok? We could break it into 70 or 80 smaller ones, and call it a a Cockaplex. Or or a porn theatre, all right? With beautiful young roachettes on stage shaking their antennae and showing off their egg sacs. But that's it.

STEW: You don't understand, without this my life has no meaning.

JOE: Oh, come on.

STEW: This is why I survived. I know it.

JOE: Don't be dramatic.

STEW: I'm gonna go electrocute myself on the smoke machine.

JOE: Stew.

STEW: I am. That would be a fitting end, I'll fry myself with the others. If this theatre doesn't survive than I don't. And don't forget who saved who earlier today. [*He runs off. He shrieks and moans. Shrieks and moans again.*]

JOE: Ok.

STEW: [*He runs back.*] Yes?

JOE: Ok ok.

STEW: Yes!!

JOE: God, all these years I thought you were just a regular roach. Who knew?

STEW: Oh, you won't regret it.

JOE: We'll see about that. So, now what, I mean look at this place, how are we gonna run it?

STEW: Well, well … how many kids do you have?

JOE: I don't know, a few hundred, you?

STEW: The same.

JOE: So?

STEW: Interns!

JOE: Right.

STEW: But my first job as artistic director is to name it. What do you think?

JOE: I don't know. How bout Manhattan Roach Club?

STEW: Hmm. Too commercial.

JOE: Lincoln Center Roaches?

STEW: Too overseas.

JOE: Cockroach Horizons?

STEW: Too past its prime.

JOE: Circle Roach Rep?

STEW: Oh no, bad karma there.

JOE: Ensemble Roach Theatre?

STEW: Too psychotic.

JOE: Atlantic Roaches?

STEW: Too robotic.

JOE: Naked Roaches?

STEW: You're kidding, right?

JOE: There'd be good parties.

[STEW *shakes his head no.*]

Insert name of the theatre where the play is being performed - Roaches?

STEW: Hmm. Doesn't ring a bell.

JOE: Well, geez I don't know.

STEW: How bout Joe's Theatre?

JOE: Hmm. How bout Joe and Stew's Theatre?

STEW: How bout Joe and Stew's Theatre of Brotherly Love.

JOE: And Financial Success. Hey, I like that.

STEW: Me too.

CRITIC: [*Off.*][*Moans.*]

JOE: What's that?

STEW: Oh God.

JOE: Oh no.

STEW: It's the

JOE: Critic!

STEW: He's mutated. He's huge!

CRITIC: [*Off.*][*Makes indistinguishable sounds.*]

JOE: What's he saying?

STEW: He's thanking God for the bomb, [*More critic sounds.*] that the director and the writer got what they deserved, [*Critic sounds.*] that he's gonna
run this place himself and do his favorite shows over and over like *The
Tale of the Allergist's Wife* and *Mnemonic*, [*Critic sounds.*] and anything
directed by someone named Scott.

JOE AND STEW: [*Scream in horror.*] Ahh!

JOE: He's coming our way. We better run.

STEW: I'm not running, this is our home. He can it have over my dead body.

JOE: This is no time for idealism.

STEW: Some things you just gotta stand up for.

JOE: Oh, brother.

STEW: Joe, he's not just a critic.

JOE: He's not?

STEW: No, he represents all the negative forces trying to beat us down, take away our creative spontaneity, and make us feel hopeless and alone. He's the bug in grade school that made fun of the way you scampered, the politician that got elected on hate and fear, the punk that stole your ice cream. Come on, this is the first day of the new world, a chance that'll never come again. Stand still and be counted. He may be big, but we have right against his might. We are brothers for art.

JOE: That's a little corn ball, isn't it?

STEW: It was from their last Christmas play, terrible writing, but it seemed apropos, and this guy gave it a good review, worst thing they did all year.

JOE: Here he comes.

STEW: Joe, are you with me?

JOE: Uh.

STEW: We've lived through it all, just like you said —

JOE: Yeah, but.

STEW: It's our theatre, not his!

JOE: It doesn't look that way.

STEW: If we don't take a stand against the critic, who will?

JOE: ... We're the only ones left.

STEW: So, are you with me, Joe?

JOE: I'm with you, Stew.

[STEW *arms himself with the toothpick.*]

STEW: Well, then. Places.

[*They head towards the stage.*]

THE END

Murray Schisgal

FIRST LOVE

Murray Schisgal

Murray Schisgal has had six plays produced on Broadway, a good many off-Broadway, Off-off Broadway, and in regional theater. He was nominated for a Tony for his play *LUV*, an Oscar for co-writing *Tootsie*, and his original TV screenplay, *The Love Song of Barney Kempinski*, ABC, '67, was nominated for Outstanding Dramatic Program. His other credits include *The Typist and the Tiger* which received the Outer Critics Circle and Vernon Rice awards. Ten of his one-act plays have been published in the *Best American Short Plays* anthologies. He is a producer of four feature films, including *A Walk On The Moon*, Miramax, and *The Devil's Arithmetic*, Showtime. In 2001, his play *Love* was successfully produced at the Comedie des Champs-Elysees in Paris, his plays *Road Show* and *A Need for Brussels* Sprouts were being performed in Tokyo, and his latest play *We Are Family* was optioned in Berlin for a production in 2002.

PLACE: LUCY ORKIN's *office on the ground floor of an East 79th Street townhouse.*

TIME: *Spring. Late day. The sky darkens during the scene.*

SOUND: *Street noises.*

AT RISE: *The office is decorated charmingly. A pine table serves as a desk; swivel chair behind it, armchair in front of it. On the right, a sofa running parallel to windows in right wall; coffee table in front of sofa; a rocking chair, upstage, facing coffee table. Rear, a small refrigerator in long cabinet on which there are books, manuscripts, files, and a Pyrex tea kettle on a hot plate. Above the cabinet are shelves also packed with books, manuscripts, framed photos and a collection of old toys. Midstage, left, is the door to the reception office.*

LUCY *is in her late thirties, an attractive, gym-fit, self-made woman, dressed simple elegance; she is wearing eyeglasses. She now paces behind desk, speaking rapidly.*

LUCY: [*Into phone.*] No, that's unacceptable. I don't know where you get your facts from, but my client's first book sold seventeen thousand in hardback and eighty-four thousand in paper; his second ... Yes, there were movie rights involved. An option was taken on it and I have every reason to believe ...

[*A beat.*]

Oliver, will you shut up for a minute! If you're not interested in the book, say so, for cryin'-out-loud, and stop wasting my time! We're talking here of an established writer who has given four years of his life to write ...

[*A beat.*]

All right, you made your point. Now see if you can follow this: If you don't accept the terms I outlined in my letter of the third by close of day Friday, I'll consider it a pass and take it elsewhere!

[*She slams phone into cradle. Then she sits behind desk, picks up last half of a sandwich, but before she can bite into it, the phone rings. She snaps it up, presses line button, and speaks into phone.*] Yes? I'll take it, Adam. [*Pressing line button, coldly.*] Why the call, Natasha?

[*A beat.*]

I thought I made myself perfectly clear. No. I don't want to represent you anymore. Don't ... [*She empties table-size Perrier bottle into glass.*] Natasha, there are other agents in town who'd be ... No! You listen to me now! When I tell a client not to speak to anyone until I've completed negotiations and that client proceeds to carry-on behind my back ...

[*A notch higher.*]

Natasha, you had no business speaking to his lawyer about anything! I've spent months bringing this deal to fruition and you've managed to destroy it with a single telephone call!

[*A beat.*]

No! My advice is to get yourself another agent!

[*She slams phone into cradle. She is breathless, palpitating. She takes two pills from a prescription container, swallows them with a drink of mineral water. She feels a bit better. She is about to reach for half of sandwich when the phone rings. She glances at her wristwatch. She expects this call. She picks up the phone, presses private line number.*] [*Into phone.*] You're late, sweetheart.

[*A beat.*]

I've been thinking about you, too.

[*A beat.*]

No, I missed lunch. I'm having a bite now.

[*A beat.*]

I decided to go to Roxbury, late Friday. Of course you're invited, but I have a load of work to do. I can't promise I'll have time.

[*Another line rings.*]

[*Into phone.*] Hold on. [*Presses another line number.*] Yes, Adam?

[*A beat; incredulously.*]

Adam, are you ... ?

[*A beat.*]

No, no, I'll see him. But keep him out there a minute. And hold my calls. [*Connects back.*] Schuyler? Well, this I can't believe. This is the most incredible ... My ex-husband is in the reception office.

[*A beat.*]

What's so extraordinary? Darling, I haven't seen or spoken to the man ... It'll be ... Don't think too harshly of me. It'll be twenty years this June 9th.

[*A beat.*]

I have no idea what he's been doing. I heard he remarried and moved somewhere out west.

[*There's a timid knock on the door.*]

[*Into phone.*] He's here! He's coming sweetheart. Yes, yes, I love you, too. I'll talk to you later. Pray for me, sweetheart. [*She hangs up; removes eyeglasses; brushes back hair, pulls down on blouse; sits upright, formally.*] Come in!

[MIKE ORKIN *enters. He's been chafed and ruddied by the raw weather. His clothes, mismatched pants and double-breasted jacket, are second-hand castoffs; he wears a black, Los Angeles baseball cap. He pushes in front of him a supermarket shopping cart, filled with deposit cans and bottles in trans-*]

parent bags. It takes him a beat or two to set the cart in a place and position that is satisfactory to him.]

LUCY: [*In amazement.*] Mike? Mike Orkin? Is that you?

MIKE: [*Almost shyly.*] Hello, Lucy. How's it been going?

LUCY: Fine, but ... What happened?

MIKE: I got married again.

LUCY: I know that. I mean ...

MIKE: My present situation?

LUCY: You don't have to answer if it makes you feel uncomfortable.

MIKE: No, no, it's okay. It's ... It's a long story, but to cut it short ... I had a couple of bad breaks. I've been living on the streets for the last few years.

LUCY: I am sorry.

MIKE: Don't be. It's not that bad a life. Especially in the fall. When the leaves begin to change their colors. [*He is straightening bags in cart.*]

LUCY: Then you're all right?

MIKE: Oh, yeah. I'm doing okay. I don't expect to be on the streets much longer. I have plans, plenty of ideas about the future. I haven't been wasting my ... [*Interrupts himself.*] You look beautiful, Lucy. It's hard to believe that we were both in the same bed together.

LUCY: It is hard to believe, Mike. Do we have to talk about it?

MIKE: You were my wife. We can't change history.

LUCY: No, we can't. But we can change the subject.

MIKE: Okay, you got it. Boy, this is something, for the two of us to be together again, after all these years. [*He sits in armchair; crosses leg, bounces it up and down, looks about, whistles; suddenly.*]   That reminds me. Where do you cash in deposit bottles in this neighborhood?

LUCY: Deposit bottles?

MIKE: Yeah. I have a lot of deposit bottles and cans in my shopping cart. Do you know a store where I can cash them in?

LUCY: Not personally, but I could ask my girlfriend, Marguerite. She works in the Mayor's office.

MIKE: Nah. Forget it. I'll find out. Parenthetically, what are you doing with that empty Perrier bottle on your desk?

LUCY: Uhhh, I haven't decided yet. Would you like me to decide now?

MIKE: I'd appreciate it. Perrier is my favorite deposit bottle.

LUCY: Then, please, be my guest.

MIKE: Thanks. [*He puts Perrier bottle into jacket pocket.*] You know, you were always generous; that was your basic nature, generosity.

LUCY: It was my basic nature. What a sicko I was.

MIKE: Frankly, I don't remember much about our marriage. But your generosity, that I remember. [*Points.*] Do you have any particular plans for that sandwich on your desk?

LUCY: Plans?

MIKE: I was wondering what you were going to do with it.

LUCY: I was going to eat it.

MIKE: [*Crestfallen.*] Oh.

LUCY: Are you disappointed in me?

MIKE: It's your sandwich.

LUCY: Yes, it is. I bought it with my own credit card.

MIKE: What kind of sandwich is it?

LUCY: Caviar and Vidalia onion.

MIKE: [*An outburst.*] Caviar and Vidalia onion! [*Whips baseball cap off his head.*] I love caviar and Vidalia onion! Caviar and Vidalia onion happens to be my favorite sandwich!

LUCY: That's incredible!

MIKE: [*Baseball cap into jacket pocket.*] Why is it incredible?

LUCY: Caviar and Vidalia onion happens to be my favorite sandwich!

MIKE: It is?

LUCY: It is! It is!

MIKE: You know what?

LUCY: What? What?

MIKE: I also love tuna fish and beefsteak tomato!

LUCY: You do? You do?

MIKE: Do you?

LUCY: I'm craaaazy about tuna fish and beefsteak tomato. In fact, I'm having tuna fish and beefsteak tomato for lunch tomorrow!

MIKE: You are?

LUCY: I are! I are!

MIKE: Jeez, unfortunately, I don't know if I'll be in the neighborhood tomorrow. In my line of business, you can't predict where you're going to be from one day to the next.

LUCY: That is unfortunate. Mike, if I gave you the last half of my caviar and Vidalia onion sandwich, would you regret leaving me and marrying another woman?

MIKE: It's your sandwich.

LUCY: Go ahead. Take it. Let's call it a belated thank-you for an uncontested divorce.

MIKE: You're a saint, Luce. A genuine saint. [*He pushes the sandwich into his mouth.*]

LUCY: Oh, I'm not a saint. You don't have to call me a saint. It's embarrassing. I'm just an ordinary, run-of-the-mill kind of girl who, after her husband left her in the middle of the night without a note or a good-bye, went on to become very rich, very successful and very, very happy. [*Shrugs.*] That's all I am. [*She rises, moves upstage and pours herself a cup of tea.*]

MIKE: You don't have to convince me. What you did, starting out at the bottom and building up your own literary agency, the biggest and the best in the city, that took some doing.

LUCY: It certainly did.

MIKE: I'm exceedingly proud to be your ex-husband.

LUCY: You certainly should be.

MIKE: It gives me goose-pimples when I see the name Orkin in a newspaper or a magazine. How come you kept my name?

LUCY: Superstition, mostly. I started my career with the name Orkin. I didn't want my luck to change.

MIKE: You want to hear something funny? I don't even remember how long ago it was when we broke up. Dates and anniversaries ... They're all a blank to me.

LUCY: You walked out on me twenty years ago, June 9th to be precise, the day after my birthday.

MIKE: It was that long ago, huh?

LUCY: Yes, it was. I had to hire a private investigator to find you so I could file for divorce.

MIKE: How do you like that. Twenty years ago. Boy, time sure flies.

LUCY: Would you like a cup of herb tea?

MIKE: What kind do you have?

LUCY: [*Reads contents on box.*] Let me see.   Red Zinger, Sleepytime, Chamomile, Grandma's Tummy Mint, Strawberry Kiwi, and ... Mandarin Orange.

MIKE: Do you have decaf Cinnamon Apple Spice?

LUCY: [*Nonplused.*] No, I don't.

MIKE: Thanks, anyway. But you have to be careful when it comes to herb teas. Some of them have more caffeine than coffee. Incidentally, how long were we married?

LUCY: [*Moves to sit on sofa, tea cup in hand.*] Nine months and fourteen days.

MIKE: We weren't even married a year?

LUCY: Nope. Not even a year. I was only eighteen. You were twenty-two.

MIKE: [*In amazement.*] I got married to you when I was only twenty-two?

LUCY: That's right.

MIKE: What the hell was my hurry?

LUCY: You said you loved me so much it hurt you.

MIKE: I said that?

LUCY: Uh huh. You also said you didn't want to set the world on fire. You just wanted to put a flame in my heart.

MIKE: I can't believe I said those lines. I had a greater facility for language than that.

LUCY: You said they were lyrics from a song your mother used to sing to you when you were a baby.

MIKE: That's possible. But I still can't believe I got married when I was twenty-two years old. [MIKE *rises, moves to rear where he looks about for something to eat. He opens refrigerator, takes out a Pyrex bowl filled with some kind of appetizer. He hunts for a fork.*] What did I know about life, about love, about interpersonal relationships? Didn't my parents object to the marriage? Didn't they raise any obstacles?

LUCY: Nope. They approved. They were at the wedding.

MIKE: Boy, my memory is like a sieve. Where did we have the wedding?

LUCY: At Bill and Janet Roberts' apartment. On Barrow Street. We had about fifty guests.

MIKE: Did we get any presents?

LUCY: A coffee-maker, a bone-handle carving set, a wooden pair of book-ends, and one thousand, two-hundred and forty-seven dollars in cash.

MIKE: Wow. That's not bad. Not bad at all. What did we do with all that money?

LUCY: We spent it. Every penny. On our honeymoon. We went to Mexico and had three marvelous weeks there.

MIKE: Good for us. [*He eats first forkful of the food in Pyrex bowl.*] Hmmm, this is delicious. Did you make it? What is it, chopped herring?

LUCY: [*Puzzled.*] Mike ...

MIKE: [*Eats another forkful.*] It's positively the best appetizer ...

LUCY: Mike, I don't want to upset you, but ... You're eating Juliet's dinner.

MIKE: Who's Juliet?

LUCY: My cat.

[MIKE's *cheeks are distended with unswallowed food. He turns upstage and expectorates the food into bowl. He then drops the bowl into a kitchen step-on lidded receptacle. He takes a can of Coke from the cabinet and moves down to sit in rocking chair where he gargles with Coke before swallowing the soda.*]

Do you remember where we met, Mike?

MIKE: Sorry. It's all a blank to me.

LUCY: I was going to NYU, and one afternoon I was sitting on a bench, in Washington Square Park, reading a book on existentialism. You sat down next to me. We talked about the book. You knew the writings of Camus, Sartre, Heidegger, Kierkegaard ... I was spellbound and you were brilliant.

MIKE: I was probably showing off.

LUCY: You told me you were writing your first novel and ... We talked and talked, and soon we were telling each other our deepest, darkest secrets, our most private, private thoughts, for hours and hours, far into the night and into the next day and the next and ... a week later I moved in with you and two months later we were married.

MIKE: It sounds romantic.

LUCY: It was. While it lasted.

MIKE: Why did we break up, Luce? What went wrong?

LUCY: You drank a great deal then. Are you still drinking?

MIKE: No more. After I became homeless I finally got smart. I haven't had any booze in over a year.

LUCY: Good for you. Anyway, you were drinking and you were having trouble writing your novel and we started fighting ...

MIKE: There was a lot of pressure on me with that novel.

LUCY: ... and quarreling and ... It was horrible. That's when I got a job at Curtis Brown. Thanks to you. But you resented my being in the publishing business. You accused me of being too ambitious, too greedy, too ... whatever. And there was something else. All of a sudden you wanted us to have kids.

MIKE: That I remember. A family, I wanted. And I wanted to get out of the city, live someplace where you could breathe fresh air and look out the window at snow-capped mountains.

LUCY: And I wanted the exact opposite: the city, a career, a weekend place in Connecticut. And I have it, Mike. I have it all now.

MIKE: You did better than I did, except ... I have three kids. Two boys and a girl.

LUCY: That's wonderful. I'm glad for you. Where did you end up living?

MIKE: Oregon. Outside Portland. Beautiful country. A lot of mountains up there. A lot of mountains. You can't walk half a mile without bumping into a mountain.

LUCY: Did you finish the novel?

MIKE: Nope. I dropped it. Everybody was expecting me to write some kind of masterpiece. I used to get sick over it. [*Rises; moves to his cart, puts empty Perrier bottle into plastic bag; finishes Coke, puts that in as well.*] Besides, after I got married, I started having new problems. I couldn't keep a job. My wife, my ex-wife now, she married a police officer a while back ... The two of us never hit it off. Don't laugh, but I came to the conclusion that I wasn't made for living in the country. I couldn't stand looking at those mountains any more, so ... I took to the road again. You were right, Lucy. The city's the only decent place to live for people like us. Did you ... ever remarry?

LUCY: If there are no surprises, I'll be married this summer.

MIKE: That's great. Congratulations. What does the guy do?

LUCY: He's a producer. Broadway musicals, mostly. [*Rises to pour more tea for herself.*]

MIKE: Couldn't you do any better? Those Broadway musicals are the worst garbage ...

LUCY: Stop that now. You don't know anything about it. Schuyler Knitsberg is an enormously successful ...

MIKE: One second, one second. What did you say his name is?

LUCY: Schuyler Knitsberg.

MIKE: His mother gave him that name?

LUCY: Mike, I'm warning you ...

MIKE: Okay, okay, that's his problem. [*He picks up framed photo from desk.*] Is this him with you?

LUCY: [*Sits in rocking chair.*] Yes, it is.

MIKE: I bear him no ill will, Luce, and I sincerely wish you two the best of everything.

[*Studies photo.*] Maybe it's wrong of me to say this as a homeless person, but ... [*Indignantly.*] ... a striped, regimental tie does not go with a glen plaid suit! I'm sorry. They do not go together. It's a grotesquery.

LUCY: I'll tell him of your sartorial criticism when I see him. I'm sure he'll take it to heart.

MIKE: I'll admit he's a pretty good looking man, although he does look pretty young to me. I'd say he's ...

LUCY: [*Without looking at him.*] Twenty-seven.

MIKE: [*Dumb struck.*] You are marrying a man of twenty-seven years of age?

[LUCY *doesn't respond.*]

Aren't you ashamed of yourself?

LUCY: Mike, if you continue ...

MIKE: I'll just say this and I'm finished.

LUCY: You will be, I guarantee it.

MIKE: When you're ninety years of age ...

LUCY: [*Through clenched teeth.*] Michael ...

MIKE: [*In one swoop.*] ... you'll be married to a kid of seventy-eight! I'm sorry. It's abnormal.

LUCY: [*Rises.*] All right, that's it! If you came by to say hello, you've said it. I have work to do. [*Sits behind desk; ready to go back to work.*]

MIKE: I knew we'd get into this sooner or later. Okay. I did come up for a reason. I ... [*A deep breath.*] Luce, I want you to be my agent; represent me; get me a contract with a publisher.

LUCY: A contract for what?

MIKE: A book. The story of my life.

LUCY: Are you serious?

MIKE: I couldn't write fiction, but I know I can write non-fiction, especially about my own life. I'll need ... uhhh ... at least five thousand dollars in advance, an assistant for research and an office to work in.

LUCY: I don' t ...

MIKE: I could do it for less. Let's say ...

LUCY: That's not the point. It's ... not practical.

MIKE: Luce, this isn't a vanity project. My life has been filled with an unbelievable number of adventures and events and ... relationships. [*Increasing fervor.*]   There are things I've experienced, things I've seen, poverty as a kid in Brooklyn, hitchhiking across country when I was seventeen, working as a dishwasher in Miami, sleeping in bus depots and train stations, pushing a hand truck in the garment district during the day and going to City College during the night ...

LUCY: Mike, that's enough. I ...

MIKE: I didn't even reach describing the years I spent as a homeless person, which are filled with innumerable adventures and ...

LUCY: Mike, that's enough.

MIKE: You have to be flexible here, Luce. This book is important to me.

LUCY: I'll give you the money you need, to get started, but as for being your agent, the answer has to be no.

MIKE: Can't you at least …

LUCY: Please, don't ask.

MIKE: I'm asking! What the hell is the big deal about it?

LUCY: If you want me to spell it out for you, I will. I don't handle unpublished authors, be they former husbands or not. And, frankly, you have no credibility as a writer. End of discussion!

MIKE: You're still angry with me for walking out on you, that's why you're turning me down.

LUCY: That's ludicrous. For your information, I don't permit my emotions to interfere with my business decisions.

MIKE: Have you become so hard, so tough, that you can treat me as if I was a stranger?

LUCY: Does that surprise you? Do you think you're more than a stranger to me? And as for becoming hard and tough … Yes, that I will attribute to your walking out on me. I had to change. To survive. To feed and clothe myself. I took a pathetically naive, young girl and made her into what you see in front of you today: a woman who is, to use your own words, too ambitious, too greedy to be tolerant of anyone's betrayal!

[*The phone rings. She snaps it up.*]

[*Into phone.*] Adam, I told you … who? All right, I'll take it. And you can put through my other calls now. I've just finished my meeting with Mr. Orkin. [*Presses another line; paces at side of desk.*] Don't you dare say a single word to me, Guido. I told you … No! Not true! I specifically told you not to show Kogan's book to anyone! That obviously included TV networks and … [*Into phone.*] [*A beat.*] I'm not interested. The deal is dead, kaput! [*She slams phone into cradle; hyperventilates.*

She takes two pills, swallows them with water. To MIKE.] It was naive of
you to walk in after so many years and expect a ... cordial welcome.
[*Sits behind desk; puts on eyeglasses; glances through contracts.*] You'll have
to forgive me, I do have a lot to do.

MIKE: So do I. I have plenty to do myself. I ... I have to go. You'll have
to excuse me. [*Puts on baseball cap.*]

LUCY: Will you let me loan you some money?

MIKE: It's not necessary. I'm fine. Thanks, anyway. [*Opens reception door.*]
Who knows, maybe I'll see you around again. But if I don't ... my
best wishes and ... you stay healthy. [*He pushes cart towards open door.*]

LUCY: Michael?

[*He turns to her.*]

Are you sure?

MIKE: I'm sure. Incidentally, you weren't eighteen when we were married. You were twenty. And I wasn't twenty-two. I was close to twenty-
five. And we weren't married nine months and fourteen days. I left
you on June 29th, not June 9th. So we were married ten months and
four days. And we didn't get one thousand, two hundred and forty-
seven dollars in cash for our wedding. We got one thousand, two hundred and seven dollars in cash. Unless you held back forty dollars.
Hasta la vista.

[*He exits, closing door. As soon as he's gone, Lucy taps out a phone number.*]

LUCY: [*Into phone.*] He just left, sweetheart. It was ... I'm still in a state
of shock. He's living on the streets.

[*A beat.*]

I am not kidding. Why would I ... ?

[*A beat.*]

That's right. A homeless person. He has a shopping cart that he seems inordinately fond of. And he collects deposit bottles. [*Annoyed.*] For the deposits, what else!

[*A beat.*]

I'm sorry, dear. I didn't mean to shout. I'm so rattled, I ... Can you imagine what it's like having your ex-husband walk into your office pushing a shopping cart and wearing a Los Angeles baseball cap? Yes, Los Angeles!

[*A beat.*]

May I ask you a question, dear? Why did your mother name you Schuyler? Did she think it went with Knitsberg?

[*A beat.*]

No, no. I'm not saying your mother is incompetent. I'm just curious. Forget it, forget it.

[*A beat.*]

I'd love to meet you for a drink. [*Glances at wristwatch.*] I'll leave in five minutes. At the Monkey Bar. Yes. I won't be late. Phone before you leave the office.

[*A beat.*]

Love you, too. [*She disconnects; presses another line.*] Adam, is Mr. Orkin still out there? Send him in. No calls.

[*She hangs up. There's a knock on the door.*]

[*Removes eyeglasses.*] Come in.

MIKE: [*Enters; without cart.*] Did you want to see me?

LUCY: Yes. I've been thinking ... Perhaps I do owe you more of an expla-
nation. I may be ... tough, Mike, but I'm not rude. Sit down, please.

[MIKE *sits in armchair; he yanks off baseball cap.*]

Publishing ain't what it used to be. It's all done by the numbers now.
How many copies did the writer's last book sell, and to what degree
is the writer known to the public by dint of murder, mayhem, or sexual perversion. It has nothing to do with a book's prose, content, or
originality.

MIKE: I didn't come to put you through any trouble.

LUCY: I'd represent you, I would, but I believe it would be impossible to
find a publisher for you.

MIKE: I know this sounds ... naive, but ... once in a while, they do pub-
lish new writers.

LUCY: Of course. It happens so rarely, though ...

MIKE: Luce, I have lived an extraordinary life. I personally traveled to
some of the least explored areas in northern California, Oregon and
Washington State. I have had relationships with a multiplicity of indi-
viduals, each relationship a story unto itself. And I have lived, deeply
and profoundly, one particular story, a love story, that haunts me every
day I walk on this earth.

LUCY: Mike ...

MIKE: Why don't you let me finish?

LUCY: [*Glances at wristwatch.*] I would, but I do have an appointment ...

MIKE: How come you didn't ask me why I left you? Why I walked out
in the middle of the night without leaving a note or even saying
good-bye? Don't you want to know?

LUCY: I did. For many years. There's no curiosity left in me.

MIKE: If I thought an apology for anything I did could make it right with you …

LUCY: [*Rises, turns on light.*] When I woke up that morning … and you weren't in the apartment … I thought you must have gone down to buy croissants or those delicious cinnamon sweet rolls we used to like, so I decided, while you were gone, to prepare for you the most splendiferous breakfast in the whole, wide world. So I put out the eggs and the butter and the bacon … And you have to believe me, Mike, I prepared for you the most extravagant, the most absolutely splendiferous breakfast conceived by the human imagination. [*Melodramatically.*] But … what's going on here? You were nowhere in sight! You were tardy, late, delinquent! The king is lost in the realm! Did you not go to the bakery? I looked in the closet. There were your clothes, the one suit, the one baseball jacket, the sweater, the pairs of pants, one brown, one blue … [*Acting panicky.*] What is going on here? An hour gone by. An hour and ten minutes. An hour and twenty minutes. An hour and … What could possibly have happened to that man? Heavens-to-Betsy, this is a frightening occurrence! I ran out towards the West Side highway. I ran into the bakery and the stores we shopped at. "Did you, perchance, see my husband? Was my husband in here? You know my husband, don't you? The dark-haired, handsome man with the eyes that sparkle and a smile that could break your heart? Did you perchance see him? … . No, no, we didn't see him. We know your husband, Mrs. Orkin. He's the best. He's the tops. He was in here yesterday and sang for us 'Che gelida manina' and he was so funny he had us all in stitches, he had us doubled over with cramps! Oh, we wouldn't forget it if we saw your husband, Mrs. Orkin. There's no one like him. No one … in the … in the whole … wide … world."

[*Her eyes are filled with tears; no sobs.*]

MIKE: Luce, I was a boozer, a drunk. I had no …

LUCY: [*Fiercely.*] Don't you tell me that! Don't you dare excuse your behavior! That! is unforgivable! That! I will not allow you! I will … [*She sobs.*] … not. I will not. No. I will not allow you …

[MIKE *rises and moves to her. He holds her, at first tentatively, but then tightly. Soon she steps back, out of his arms and wipes her eyes with a hand-*

kerchief; she turns to stare out the window. Darkness has descended. Faint sounds of street noises. The phone rings, three times, and stops. Neither one is brought out of the moment.]

MIKE: I had no ... control ... over myself. Or what I did. Or how I acted. Not because I was a drunk. It wasn't that. I was afraid, Luce. Panic-stricken. Not conscious of any feelings except ... self-disgust.

[*A beat.*]

I couldn't live with you any more. I couldn't look at you, be with you, share anything with you. We were ... terminally incompatible. You were so ... energetic, so ... filled with your marriage, me, your career, your friends, your future. The sun was always out for you. Even at midnight. It reflected in your eyes so that I couldn't look at them without turning away.

[*A beat.*]

Bill Roberts said to me, "She's got it, Mike. In five years, she'll be one of the hottest agents in the city. There's no one around like her."

[*A beat.*]

There wasn't. I knew it. And I never loved you as much as when I left you. But I had to go. It wasn't anything I planned. I had no control, Luce. I just ran, in a panic. I ran out the door and I said to myself, I'll die before I come back here! I'll die, I swear!" Because ... Because the alternative to leaving was staying, was having you look at me, watch me, see me with your sun-filled eyes ... and be humiliated by my insurmountable deficiencies ... by my ... irreversible failures.

[*A beat.*]

But I never really left you. Never. A day of my life hasn't passed without me touching your hair, smelling the fragrance of your body, feeling you close to me.

LUCY: [*Turns to him.*] Is that the love story you want to write?

MIKE: It's the only one I know.

[*Their eyes hold a beat. Lucy moves to sit on sofa.*]

LUCY: Why won't you borrow some money from me?

MIKE: I can't.

LUCY: Then I guess I'll just have to be your agent and try my damndest to get someone interested in your book.

MIKE: That's all I ask.

LUCY: How long have you been in the city?

MIKE: Three, four months.

LUCY: What brought you here today?

MIKE: Good question.

LUCY: Is there an answer?

[MIKE *seems to be somewhere inside himself.*]

LUCY: [*Cont'd.*] Mike?

[*He looks at her.*]

What brought you here today?

MIKE: I had an unexpected discovery.

LUCY: What was it?

MIKE: It's not anything ... [*A breath.*] A couple of days ago, I found this ... [*Presses his fingers beneath his arm.*] ... bump under my arm. I went to the clinic at St. Claire's this morning. I have an appointment to go back. Tomorrow. For a biopsy. [*Uncertainly.*] It's no big deal. I just wanted to see you ... about my book.

LUCY: Sit here, Mike.

[*He sits beside her on sofa. Lucy smiles.*]

LUCY: [*Cont'd.*] It is nice seeing you again, Mr. Orkin.

MIKE: I'm glad to be with you again, Mrs. Orkin.

LUCY: Do you remember our honeymoon in Mexico?

MIKE: Oaxaca.

LUCY: What do you remember about it?

MIKE: We were together. We were young.

LUCY: And?

MIKE: What?

LUCY: Everybody was in love with us.

MIKE: Even the donkeys.

LUCY: Especially the donkeys.

MIKE: We had fun, didn't we?

LUCY: More fun than I let myself remember.

MIKE: I never wanted to hurt you.

LUCY: I know.

[*A beat.*]

By the way, I just thought of an editor at HarperCollins who'd be interested in your book. It's not going to be a problem. And you were right. The bump under your arm ... It's no big deal. They do a biopsy on everything nowadays. There's no reason to worry.

MIKE: I'm not worried. If it was serious, they wouldn't have been so casual about it.

LUCY: Of course not.

MIKE: They would have taken a biopsy right then and there. They would have kept me for observation.

LUCY: Absolutely. They're not inhuman.

MIKE: I am tired, Luce. I do feel ... very tired.

LUCY: When was the last time you had a good night's sleep?

MIKE: It's hard to sleep in a shelter. There's always something going on there.

LUCY: [*Rises.*] Then why are you surprised you're tired? Come on, take off your shoes. [*She packs a pillow against upstage arm of the sofa.*] You'll nap for an hour and you'll feel a thousand percent better.

[MIKE *doesn't move.*]

Go ahead, take them off. I don't have all night. I'm supposed to be meeting someone right now for a drink. I don't even know what I'm doing here.

[MIKE *pulls off his shoes.*]

Now your jacket. You don't expect to be comfortable sleeping in your jacket, do you? [*She helps him remove his jacket.*] You really have let yourself go to pot. I don't understand how you could have ... [*She drops what would have been a reprimand.*] You'll have an office here. I'll arrange for you to meet the applicants so you can choose your own secretary. Don't think having me for an agent is going to be a picnic. You don't know how really tough I can be. You'll probably be sorry you ever came. Well, go ahead, lie down, what are you waiting for?

MIKE: My life will make a good book, won't it?

LUCY: Your life will make a terrific book. You haven't lived one life, you've lived ten lives. Just focus on what brought you back to writing after spending years as a homeless person. That's the stuff that makes for best sellers.

MIKE: Thanks, Luce. For your support. And for being such a generous person.

LUCY: That's my nature.

[*Their eyes hold a beat longer.* MIKE *lies down on sofa, turning towards window, his back to* LUCY, *his hands under cheek, his knees bent.*]

[LUCY *opens a paisley shawl and covers him with it. The phone rings.* LUCY *turns to stare at it. Then turns to stare at* MIKE. *The phone continues ringing.*]

Move over, old man. I'm getting tired, too.

[*And she lies down on sofa, facing* MIKE's *back. She presses close to him, her knees fitting into the underside of his knees. She hugs him tightly. A pair of spoons. Wedged together. Snugly.*]

[*Lights and phone ringing fade.*]

END OF PLAY

Nicky Silver

CLAIRE

Nicky Silver

His plays include *Pterodactyls* (Oppenheimer Award, Kesselring Award, Drama Desk nomination, Outer Critic's Circle nomination), *The Eros Trilogy*, *Raised in Captivity* (Drama Desk nomination, Outer Critics Circle nomination, Drama-Logue Award), *The Food Chain* (Outer Critic's Circle nomination), *Fat Men in Skirts, Fit to be Tied, The Maiden's Prayer, Free Will & Wanton Lust* (Helen Hayes Award), *My Marriage to Ernest Borgnine* and *The Altruists.*

CLAIRE, *is seated at her armoire, powdering her face. She is gracious in the extreme.*

CLAIRE: I have, for a long time, been a person who *tries* to see the best in others. I have, always, tried to see the beauty in all things. No matter how *grotesque.*

And I find, more and more, I live in a grotesque world. Isn't everything ugly all of a sudden? I do not understand, I must admit, what passes for music in this age. But then, I force myself to remember that my mother did not understand my music, and I try to see the beauty in giving in, giving way, like a weeping willow bending gracefully in the inevitable face of gravity.

[*She glances into the mirror and is momentarily side-tracked.*]

My mother was a sad woman to begin with, and then, when I was eight years old, she lost a baby. And her sadness became exaggerated to the point of farce.

[*Returning to her point.*]

This morning, I went to the dressmaker, to be fitted for a dress. I walked to the shop. It's not very far and I enjoy what's left of the fresh air. And I enjoy seeing people. Or I did. You see, more and more people seem to feel it all right to behave anyway they choose. For instance, more and more people seem to be — How shall I put this? — *Spitting.* I do not approve of this. Sometimes they walk over to the curb and spit into the street, as if this were so much better than spitting in the middle of the pavement. It's not. And apparently plenty of people feel as I do and they spit right where they are. And not just men, but women too! With hair-dos and skirts. Now, I want to see the beauty in all of this, but it's *very* hard. It is eight blocks from my door to the dress-maker's and I must've passed thirty-five people spitting in the first three. Is it something in the air? Is it a by-product of auto exhaust that has everyone spitting so continually? Now, I am willing to blame an awful lot on the industrial revolution, but not this, this sudden spitting frenzy. No.

[*She glances at her bed, and loses her train of thought.*]

When my sister died in my mother's womb, my father buried his head in bottles and, I suspect, under the covers of strange beds.

[*Returning.*]

   At any rate, after the third block of my walk, I started counting
these people who committed what I considered were affronts against
civilization. Have we learned nothing in the past five thousand years?
Don't these *people*, these *spitters*, realize that we all have to live together,
and I would no sooner want to see their *expectorations* as I would their
bowel movements? You may think me silly, but I believe that all the wars
and suffering and prejudice and hate come down to nothing more than
an unwillingness to understand each other. If we would only allow
each other the space of our dignity, we would save so much time and
trouble, and the money that we spend on nuclear weapons could be
given to The New York City Ballet, who really do lovely work, that
no one could find fault with!
   As I was saying, I started counting "spitters." And within the
next three blocks, I counted thirteen more — well, actually I counted
fourteen. But I allowed for one man who was also muttering to himself, and barking, from time to time, like a dog. I believe this man was
suffering from, the once little-known, suddenly fashionable, disease
called *"Turette's Syndrome."* I saw a story all about it on a television
news magazine, and I was, therefore, in a position to be sympathetic.
My aesthetic is not so rigid that it doesn't allow for legitimate illness.
I have never been sick a day in my life — but when I was eighteen,
my father developed cancer of the pancreas and died. And he left me
a great deal of money.
   I don't know why my mind keeps wondering back to my parents.
It's not what I intended, because something happened this morning,
and I'm trying to get to that. But my mind keeps wondering off in
tangents. A dear friend of mine once told me I spoke in a *baroque* fash-
ion. I've no idea what she meant, but I'm sure it wasn't a compliment.
Oh well, I never liked her anyway!
   Oh, I'll get to my point, the thing that happened. I will. But right
now I can't help remembering my mother's face at my father's funeral.
It was long. She had a long face. Like a Modigliani painting. I've *never*
liked Modigliani, although I found the Off-Broadway play about him,
several seasons back, mildly entertaining. Still, I thought Mother was
lovely. She had more dimension than his paintings. And she moved.
Slowly. She possessed the grace of a ballet dancer and the alacrity of
a pachyderm — I'm using sarcasm to make a point. She was languid

in an era when things considered beautiful actually were. Before min-
imalism crept into our landscape, when we could see farther and were
unhindered by the cataract of modernism. I seem to see her all the time
as a ballet dancer, in a Degas painting. I've *always* liked Degas, and I
feel badly that they never made a play about him. But Mother was lovely.
And before "the baby," as we euphemistically referred to her miscar-
riage, she as melancholy, but serene. Her hands were white, and she
never wore nail polish. Every year at Christmas she would tie bows
on hand-made presents, her fingers dancing 'round the ribbons. And
she *worshipped* my father, who was enormous. He had to be six and a
half feet tall, with feet as big as tennis rackets. He scared me, truth be
told. He would be very quiet, but inside there was an anger, building
up, building over something, it could be anything. And then all of a
sudden he would explode! And fists went flying and plates and tem-
pers. — But he never swore. Which is odd. And makes him seem,
somehow, less masculine, in my mind. But after "the baby," things
changed *drastically*.

Mother, whom I mentioned was laconic to begin with, became
absolutely *inert*. I don't mean the days immediately following, which,
of course, she spent in bed. But the days became weeks and she
wouldn't budge. She *never* got out of bed of her own accord. After
about three weeks, we, my father and I, foisted her into a sitting position and put a book in her lap. We tilted her head so she was in a position to read. But she didn't! I sat there and stared and stared, and her
eyes never touched a word! I said to her, "Mother, why don't you read?"
...... .I do not care to. She responded. Resolutely.

Oh. Well. If she didn't care to, she didn't care to. There was
little arguing. So at day's end, we put the book on her night stand and
turned out her lamp. In the morning, we tried again. "Why don't
you read, Mother? You might enjoy it." "I do not care to."

Hmmm. After about a week of "the book game," I went with my
father into her room. We tried to interest her in getting up, getting
dressed. "I do not care to." This was a woman of definite likes and
dislikes. But my father had decided this "bed-rest thing" had gone
on long enough. Perhaps, being a woman himself and only recently
having had an unborn baby die in his belly, he felt he was the best judge.
— I'm using sarcasm to make a point. So, we lifted her out of bed.
This was easy. He was big. She was small. And he held her up, rather
like a marionette, while I dressed her. Now, I was eight, and natu-
rally jealous that I'd been replaced as the center of the house, so I put
her in a very ugly outfit! Plaid skirt, floral sweater, two different ear-

rings and so on. "We're going for a walk!" my father informed her. And she responded — exactly right! "I do not care to." But out we went and, flanked on either side, she greeted the fresh air. We looked like Oscar Levant, Fred Astair, and a drug-ridden Nannette Fabray, three strong in strides from "The Bandwagon!"

Now don't misunderstand me. She was not catatonic. No. She was not a zombie. She just chose not to. From that day on, she chose not to. We pretty much had to prop her up all over the place. We'd stand her at the stove, and she'd cook something — although her disinterest in the project usually resulted in dinners of pudding and peas. Or my favorite: Aspirin! She just reached up, into the cupboard and cooked what she grabbed.

[She is really enjoying herself.]

Oh, we'd prop her up in front of the radio. We'd put a vacuum in her hand and she's clean the same spot, over and over again ... until it was immaculate! At first, I didn't mind at all. It was like having this huge doll that really did wet herself. And I'd have my friends over after school to play with her. But, before long, I grew bored ... the way children do. And as the years passed, my father came home later and later, leaving her to me. And he never yelled anymore. And he never threw things.

By the time he died he seemed very sad. That was a terrible time, the time he died. I was eighteen — Oh, I said that. And although he left me ample money to have someone take care of her, I didn't feel I could leave my mother. Besides, I was still in high school, where I was considered very pretty and everyone liked my stories. I was *always* charming, even then. And in an era where chastity was vogue, I was liberal with my favors. I was very popular with any number of young men attending NYU and Columbia, and even as far away as Princeton. It wasn't that I liked sex so much. Because I didn't. Then. I don't know. I was too giggly to really dictate what I wanted. And besides, that was unheard of then.

[With authority.]

Women today are very lucky that it's become fashionable to actually indicate to their bed partners the location of their clitoris — excuse me, EXCUSE ME, but it's true. But I was never stupid. And

I saw me peccadilloes as escape routs. Remember, I was still prop-
ping her up and picking her clothes and cooking for her, unless I was
willing to dine on Ajax, which she took to incorporating into her recipes
the way homemakers on a budget work with tuna.

The point is, I quickly became pregnant. I never took precau-
tions, knowing little about them, and wouldn't if I'd known more. I
didn't see a doctor. I didn't have to. I knew it. I could feel it. So, I
spent the next week dating the seven candidates who might be my baby's
father. A couple, I was sure, would softly hold my hand all the way
to their Park Avenue doctors to have my ticket to freedom scraped
from inside me. But Philip was, then, a gentle man. And I could tell
when he looked at me that he adored me. Even if I couldn't tell when
we made love. So the following week, I informed him that I was carrying his child, and true to form, he asked me to marry him.

Three months later, my mother who'd really deserted me ten years
earlier, deserted me finally. She died of a stroke in mid-afternoon.
She should have been dressed. She could have been up and doing
things. But, I assume ... she did not care to.

I thought of leaving Philip, since I'd married him to escape my
life, which now escaped me. But I was pregnant and he was wealthy
and solicitous. In time, I had Philip, whom I loved. And Amy, whom
I did not. I don't know why. Perhaps it's because she's such a grace-
ful and delicate flower — I use sarcasm to illustrate myself.

Children are an odd phenomenon, don't you find? I have to say,
I've never really understood them. It seems so irrational to me. You
create something. You carry something around, inside of you, for what
seems an eternity, and then you are delivered a person. A stranger.
And you can tell me otherwise, but from the minute we're born, we
are people. My children had likes and dislikes from day one. Philip
adored music and art and emulated me. While Amy, on the other hand,
turned her nose up at my breast and never really came around!

[*Lecturing.*]

I see young mothers in the park walking their children, like poo-
dles on leashes. I am aghast! They treat their children as if they were
objects. I claim no expertise *BUT* it has been my experience that children are not dogs. Were they dogs, I'm afraid, I'd've been tempted
to put Amy to sleep several times by now. I don't mean to be hard
about Amy. I'm sure she has many fine qualities — which are not appar-
ent to me. All people have goodness inside of them! Only some peo-

ple have very little, and it's *very*, *very*, *very* deep down. And she is a
stranger! That's what it comes down to. I know she came from me,
but she's not part of — oh, God. I must sound awful. But it's true.
My feet are part of me. My hands are part of me. My children are
people I know. I do love them. Don't mistake my objectivity for indif-
ference. I love my children very much. I just see that they are *other*
people. And, if you ask me, we'd have a great deal less crime and drug
addiction if mothers and fathers realized their children are not their
pets. And this understanding would lead to happier children, health-
ier adults, less crime, lower taxes, a thriving economy, prettier archi-
tecture, less television, more theater, less litigation, more understanding,
less alienation, more love, less hate and a calmer humanity who felt
less of a need to spit all the time in public!! Because that's what it is,
really. All this spitting in public, is just a thinly veiled hostility for ME,
MY TASTE, MY AESTHETIC AND THE COMMON CON-
SENSUS OF WHAT IS GENERALLY CONSIDERED
SOCIALLY ACCEPTABLE!! — AND ISN'T IT WONDERFUL
HOW I HAVE COME FULL CIRCLE, AND CAN NOW CON-
TINUE WITH MY STORY IN A NATURAL, LOGICAL FASH-
ION!!
       Everything goes in circles really. Except things that go in straight
lines. Hmmm.
       I was counting spitters, vile angry, lost soul who felt impotent to
change their lives in view of what they think is fate. Well, after about
a hundred of these spitting villains, I could take no more. I was in a
rage! What has happened to my lovely city! What has happened to
it? The buildings are suddenly eyesores. There are placards everywhere, for so-called bands, I've never heard of with fascist sounding
names and illustrations of women so wanton as to degrade women
everywhere.
       Finally, I could take no more. So I started following this one young
woman, who looked reasonably sane — except for the fact that she was
wearing a tweed skirt with sneakers, but I allowed for a foot condi-
tion. She had on a blazer. Her light brown hair was piled high on
her head with a tortoise clip. She looked fine. She looked normal. I
thought to myself, "I will just stare at this young woman. I will not
look to her right. I will not look to her left. I will see only her. And
I will convince myself, that I am surrounded by similarly sane young
women. I won't look, so I'll assume everyone around me is just as polite
and normal as she … .." And it was working. I had myself believing
it. Everything was lovely … .and then she *veered* over to the curb.

[A real panic builds inside of her.]

I said a silent prayer. This woman had become, to me, a symbol: the last great kindness in a once kind world. My breathing changed. I felt my hands grow tense and saw my knuckles whiten in my clenched fists. She walked along the curb for a few feet. I thought, "Thank you, God, thank you. She's just walking along the curb. She's a little erratic, but she's not one of them, she's one of us!" And then slowly, it seemed as if everything was in slow motion ... she *leaned* over. I hoped, I prayed she was going to faint! I hoped she was ill and going to die! "Let her die a martyr to beauty, but please God, *please*, don't let her spit! Let her fall over, into the street, into the traffic, let her be canonized the patron saint of civilization, but PLEASE GOD, don't let her spit!" And she made a small coughing noise. "She's coughing — you're coughing — she's coughing — aren't you? — please don't be clearing your throat — just be coughing!" If I shut my eyes, I'll miss whatever happens and I can pretend that nothing happened and I can go on, continue to live and hope! But they would not close! I couldn't shut them! I wanted to! I tried to! But I couldn't! I was hypnotized! I just stared and stared and the seconds became hours and the hours weeks and the weeks millennia! And then it happened!!!

SHE SPIT!!!

And the world went black and the sun fell out of the sky, burning the earth and sending the building tumbling, bricks flying, people crushed in the rain of debris and humanity, which had only recently learned to walk was SMASHED into oblivion for all time!! "WHAT'S WRONG WITH YOU!?" I found my hand on her sleeve. "Don't you understand what you've done?!" She spun around with such a look of utter horror and disgust on her face that I was only spurred to continue — "The world is decomposing! Humanity is rotting away! We're reverting to the behavior of apes and YOU'RE TO BLAME!" "Let go of me!!" She shouted, very loudly, much more loudly than was called for. "I had to spit. What's it to you?!" And with that she shoved me, hard, and I fell onto the pavement.

All I could think about was how sad, how sorry, I was, that I'd chosen badly, chosen someone who didn't care, couldn't be convinced, didn't see that we are all just withering, dying, crumbling in on ourselves ... I looked around from my *position* on the sidewalk and I was the center of quite a crowd. And I thought, "Oh no. I'm sitting in it. She's gone, and I am sitting in her *expectoration!*"

[*Sad and shaken.*]

And. Then. I shut my eyes and I hurried to the dressmaker. I was late of course and she was already on her next client, my old friend, Phoebe Potter. We were girls in school together. She looked so old, and I was so distraught from my experience that I mistook her for a mirror. It broke me completely, to see myself in her eyes and the folds of her flesh. "I'll come back tomorrow." "No, no. Mrs. Potter's almost finished." And so I waited … .And, soon, it was my turn.

I looked into the mirror as I was pinned. And, I was me again. I was shaken, but I was myself. I heard music in my head while she worked. And. As soon as I could, I rushed home. To Tony.

[*Quite still, forgetting herself.*]

I did not speak. I unbuttoned his shirt and he wrapped his arms around my waist, mumbling something into my ear, which I couldn't or didn't understand. Didn't care. And I filled up the palms of my hands with his shoulders. He pulled my blouse from my skirt in the back and I pressed my hips against his genitals and felt his erection, under his jeans. I kicked off my shoes and unbuttoned his pants, holding him, hardened, in my right hand and pulling his hair with my left, while he penetrated my mouth with his tongue. He unbuttoned my blouse down the back and pulled it off, lowering himself to take my nipples in his mouth, while I stroked his eyelids with my fingertips. How late in life I came to understand sex, how much time I wasted. He unfastened my skirt and it fell to the ground. I bent over and licked his ears and the back of his neck. He licked my thighs and in between. And I led him to my bed. My baby. My baby boy. And he stood over me, making me want him, and understanding that I wanted to be made to want. And we made love with the violent passion of children and animals ripping at each other, biting and hurting beautifully … .And from my bed, the window views the river and the city beyond, and as he held me, as I had him, I became a child again, the years dripping away and falling off of me, until I was a girl. And the river flowed and the city on the other side changed from what it is to what it was: the sharp angry teeth of the building, the glass angles and steel knives became rounded. Until he finished. And I finished. And I threw my head back and the sun was setting on a city of the past, where everything was beautiful, and we were children, and more … easily pleased.

[*She looks around and realizes that she has exposed more than she intended.*]

So you see, sex, it seems, is very important, when it comes to seeing the beauty of things.

[*She crosses to her dressing table, and slowly lets her hair down.*]

[*The lights fade slowly.*]

END OF PLAY

Shel Silverstein

WHAT ARE YOU DOING IN THERE?

Shel Silverstein

Shel Silverstein was last represented on the New York stage with his play *The Devil and Billy Markham*, which played a double bill with David Mamet's *Bobby Gould in Hell*, collectively titled *Oh! Hell*, at the Mitzi Newhouse Theatre at Lincoln Center. With Mr. Mamet, he co-wrote the screenplay *Things Change* for Columbia Pictures which starred Don Ameche and Joe Mantengna. His play, *Hamlet*, was performed at the Ensemble Studio Theatre in New York.

Mr. Silverstein wrote and illustrated several children's classics, including *Where The Sidewalk Ends*, *A Light in the Attic*, and *The Giving Tree*. His plays include *The Crate*, *Lady or the Tiger*, *Gorilla* and *Little Feet*. He was also a noted cartoonist and the author of many songs and poems. His song *I'm Checking Out of Heartbreak Hotel* from the film, *Postcards from the Edge*, was nominated for an Academy Award. Shel Silverstein passed away in 1999.

LEONARD *stands at the bathroom sink, downstage center. His hands are in sink. He moves them as if washing them — slowly, He does this for a while. Then there is a knocking at the door,* LEONARD *does not look up. A while later, there is another knock. Still no response.*

MOTHER'S VOICE: Leonard? [*Pause.*] Leonard? [*Pause.*] Leonard, are you coming out of there? [*Pause.*] I wish you'd come out of there. Other people have to use the bathroom. [*Pause.*] You're not the only one in this house. [*Pause.*]

FATHER'S VOICE: Leonard — [*Loud knock.*] Leonard, goddammit — Get the hell out of there — Your mother wants to get in there.

MOTHER: He can't monopolize that bathroom.

FATHER: Other people have to get in there — [*Knock.*] You're monopolizing — Are you coming out of there? You're not the only member of this family — [*Knock.*] Do you hear me? [*Pause.*]

MOTHER: Is he all right?

FATHER: He's all right — Leonard, you've got your mother worried now — Is that what you want? You want to worry everybody sick?

MOTHER: I'm not worried sick, Ben. I just wanted to — Leonard, are you all right? [*No response.*]

FATHER: [*Loud banging.*] Leonard? Leonard, will you respond, for chrissake? Will you have the decency to respond? He doesn't even have the decency to respond.

MOTHER: I just want to know you're all right. That's all I want.

FATHER: You also want to use the bathroom — We all want to use the goddamn — We've got a right to use the — [*Bang.*] Leonard? All right, how would you like me to get a screwdriver and take this door off by the hinges? How would you like that?

MOTHER: Ben — You're getting yourself worked up.

FATHER: I'm gonna get a screwdriver. I promise you I'm gonna get a screwdriver and take off the goddamn door — I promise you Leonard.

MOTHER: Leonard, you're getting your father worked up. [*Pause.*] What are you doing in there?

FATHER: I know what you're doing in there, Leonard. I'm just telling you stop it and come out and let somebody else use the bathroom.

MOTHER: What is he doing in there?

FATHER: Leonard, do you want me to get the screwdriver? Do you want me to embarrass you?

MOTHER: What is he doing in there? How do you know what he's doing?

FATHER: I know — I've been there, Leonard, There's a time to do it and a time to stop — quit — enough is enough.

MOTHER: Stop what? Is he smoking dope in there? Leonard, are you smoking dope in there?

FATHER: He's not smoking dope.

MOTHER: How do you know? How do you know what he's doing? You don't have X-ray eyes.

FATHER: If he was smoking dope you could smell it — I know what he's doing.

MOTHER: What is he doing? What?

FATHER: Figure it out — You're not a dummy — You're not a child — Figure it out, for God's sake.

MOTHER: You're not the only one with problems, Leonard, we all have problems. I have problems with my health — I don't burden you with them — I try to deal with them — Families have problems of just living together, sharing the same space — We have to make allowances. We have to make adjustments, Leonard.

FATHER: We have to let each other in the goddamn bathroom.

MOTHER: We have to recognize the needs of others. We can't be self-oriented.

FATHER: You're talking to yourself. He couldn't care less. He's not even listening.

MOTHER: Leonard, can you grasp what I'm trying to say?

FATHER: You're talking to the wall. You're talking to a door. Leonard, this is positively my last warning — I swear it — I'm trying to treat you like a man — I'm trying to afford you some common courtesy — Can you appreciate that? I'm not just banging the door down. I'm trying to let you compose yourself. Can you appreciate that?

MOTHER: He *is* Leonard. The man's trying to reason with you — Don't make him humiliate himself.

FATHER: Listen, I'm not the one who's humiliated, believe me. I'm not the one who's degraded.

MOTHER: *I* feel humiliated — Standing and begging — Leonard, can you understand that? — Standing outside a bathroom-begging someone to talk to you — Can you understand what that does to a person?

FATHER: He doesn't understand that. You're talking about other people's feelings. He has no understanding of that. I'll tell you what he understands. — [*Loud.*] I'll tell you what you understand. I'm *grounding* you — You understand that? One week — every night — grounded — totally — completely — you understand that? No car — no money — no TV. You understand? — No goddamn music — [*Silence.*]

MOTHER: Ben, I am worried. [*Knock.*] Leonard, please just tell me you hear me. He may have his earphones on.

FATHER: He hears you, for God's sake, Ella. Can't you accept the fact that he hears you and doesn't give a goddamn? — He's choosing not to respond — accept it — I'm going for the screwdriver.

MOTHER: Leonard — will you please just be —

LEONARD: I *hear* you. [*Silence.*]

MOTHER: And you're all right?

LEONARD: I'm all right, OK?

FATHER: I told you he was all right. He just does not respond to adult treatment. He has no regard for the rights of others.

MOTHER: Well, you come out when you want to — As long as we know you're all right — OK?

FATHER: When he *wants* to — He'll be in there all week pullin' that thing.

MOTHER: All right Leonard, what thing?

FATHER: Listen. [*Bang.*] Listen — *I'm* not saying stay as long as you want — Your mother said that. I'm not saying it. I'm saying get your ass out of there right now — *now* — I'm saying let it go and zip up and get the hell out here and let someone else use that john — *I* have to use the john.

MOTHER: Ben, you don't — Don't tell him you have to use the —

FATHER: I *do* — I didn't have to before but now I do! Don't tell me I don't have to — You don't know my bladder — You don't know what standing here and screaming for twenty minutes can do to my bladder or my bowels. You don't know — Leonard, are you coming out? Are you coming out? [*Bang.*]*Are* [*Bang.*] *you* [*Bang.*] *coming* [*Bang.*] out? [*Bang.*] *Are you?*

MOTHER: Just tell the man you're coming out — He's having a fit — Ben, you're having a fit.

FATHER: [*Banging.*] *Are you –Are you-Are you-Are you —*

LEONARD: I'll be right out.

MOTHER: He'll be right out.

FATHER: *When?* When will he be right out? What-is right out? — Come out now — right now.

MOTHER: He'll be right out. Give him a minute.

FATHER: *When? When?*

LEONARD: When I'm finished.

FATHER: *When?*

MOTHER: When he's *finished*, Ben.

FATHER: Finished with *what?*

MOTHER: With what?

FATHER: I know with what — I want to know when, Is that too much to ask? — I'm standing here with my bladder busting and I want to know when.

MOTHER: Tell him when, Leonard, I can't take much more of this.

FATHER: Are your pills in there?

MOTHER: I don't know.

FATHER: Leonard, your mother needs one of her pills — Will you let her in there? Will you please, in the name of God, let her in there? — [*Bang bang.*] In the name of *God!*

MOTHER: Please, Ben — Please, please, you're getting everybody sick.

FATHER: *He's* getting everybody sick — He's sick and he's making you sick.

MOTHER: *You're* making me sick and you're making yourself sick.

LEONARD: I'm almost finished. Can you hear me? — I'm almost finished.

FATHER: We've never had any trouble hearing you — We don't hear you if you don't talk. You have to speak to be heard.

MOTHER: He just spoke.

FATHER: He spoke — Hallelujah — He has spoken — the Lord has spoken.

MOTHER: He's almost finished.

FATHER: [*Mimicking.*] He's almost finished. Hooray.

MOTHER: Leonard, I'm going to fix some tomato soup — cream of tomato — Do you want some!

FATHER: Don't bribe him, for chrissake. Don't insult him.

MOTHER: I'm not insulting him. I asked him if he wanted some soup. You're getting yourself sick, Ben.

FATHER: You're insulting us all. He's insulting you and me — and *you're* insulting us all.

MOTHER: There are no insults — He's coming right out — aren't you? Aren't you, Leonard? Leonard — Almost finished.

LEONARD: [*Lifts hands from sink. They are covered with blood: He sways and puts them back in sink.*]

MOTHER: See — he's almost finished.

FATHER: I'll believe it when I see it.

[*Lights fade*]

END OF PLAY

Donald Steele

THE WAY TO MIAMI

To my parents,
Fey B. Steele and Mary Alice Steele
and
To Roger Mooney

Donald Steele

Donald Steele is a member of The Dramatists Guild and is a Fellow of the MacDowell Colony. He is a graduate of Hope College and The University of Iowa. He is also a new member of the 42nd Street Workshop. His work has been performed in New York, Chicago, and Los Angeles. His full length play *Graceland* was initially produced at American Stage festival, and has received readings across the country. He has written many one-act plays including his one-woman piece *Miracle at the Del Mar Boulevard Beauty Salon* which was originally performed by the Oscar winner Mercedes Ruehl. In 1996, *The Way to Miami* was part of the Octoberfest at Ensemble Studio Theatre. In the cast were Suzanne Shepherd and Baxter Harris. In 1998, the play was a winner in the 23rd Annual Off-Off Broadway Festival hosted by Samuel French, Inc., and was subsequently published by them. The production was produced by the Bridge Theatre Company and was directed by the playwright. In the cast were Ruth Sherman nd Ron Crawford.

CHARACTERS

FRANK: *mid 60's*
LEOLA: *his wife. 60's*

SETTING: *Frank and Leola's kitchen*

TIME: *Before dawn*

PROPERTY PLOT:
    1 table large enough to seat six
    5 chairs for the table
    1 tablecloth for the table
    5 dinner plates
    5 salad plates
    5 dessert plates
    2 coffee cups and saucers
    2 coffee mugs
    1 pot with lid
    Bubblewrap and newspapers
    Packing cartons for the dishes, tablecloth, pot and lid
    [at least six cannons - various sizes]

COSTUME PLOT
    FRANK: Casual pants; loafers or sneakers; brightly colored
        short sleeve shirt ala Hawaiian style.
    LEOLA: Slippers or casual slip ons; earrings; caftan with zipper
        or button front [not a bathrobe].

*In the dark we hear a man singing and humming a tune. The lights come up
on* FRANK, *in his sixties, sitting at a kitchen table. The kitchen is crowded with
cartons packed for moving.* FRANK *is drinking coffee from one of the two mugs
on the table and consulting a highway map. He wears a brightly colored Hawaiian
type shirt.* LEOLA *enters, also in her sixties, wearing a caftan like robe, adjust-
ing an earring. She goes to one of the packed cartons, picks it up, sets it on the
table, and begins unpacking it.*

FRANK: What are you doing?

LEOLA: Looking for a cup.

FRANK: I got cups out.

LEOLA: I want one of my nice dinner cups.

FRANK: I got out the mugs.

LEOLA: You drink it out of a mug. I want one of my nice dinner cups. Hold this.

[*She hands him a stack of plates wrapped in newspaper.*]

FRANK: Don't unpack all of this to find one cup. The movers will be here.

[*She continues handing him plates wrapped in paper. She begins to unwrap them as she goes along.*]

LEOLA: They aren't here yet. I want the last cup of coffee I'll ever drink in this house to be out of one of my nice china dinner cups. We bought that set for special occasions. This is a special occasion. Not a special one like Christmas or Thanksgiving, but I guess some people would call this a special occasion.

FRANK: A lot of people would call moving to Florida a special occasion. I do. It's not every day you move to Florida.

[LEOLA *hands him another stack of plates.*]

LEOLA: Here. Unwrap these.

FRANK: These are plates. You wanted a cup.

LEOLA: I want to look at the plates again.

FRANK: Why?

LEOLA: I'm going to re-wrap them. I don't like how I wrapped them.

FRANK: You wrapped them just fine.

LEOLA: It's been plaguing me. I want to re-wrap them again.

FRANK: You're making a mess.

LEOLA: We're moving. We have an excuse. What are a few wrinkled papers?

FRANK: A few?

[LEOLA *hands him another stack of plates.*]

LEOLA: How many is that there?

FRANK: If you wanted to drink your coffee out of one of those nice cups, why'd you pack it?

LEOLA: It crossed my mind, but I thought, "Don't be stupid." I felt silly. Is that five of everything there?

[FRANK *looks to count. So does she.*]

FRANK: One. Two. Three. Four. Five. Yes. Five. Why?

LEOLA: You. Me. Joanna. Gloria. And Jimmy. Where's a tablecloth?

FRANK: For what?

LEOLA: I want to set the table one more time.

FRANK: Set the table? Now? I told the movers we'd be all ready.

LEOLA: We are.

FRANK: We were. Now we aren't. This is not ready.

LEOLA: So are they pulled up out front? No. Where's the box I put the tablecloths in?

FRANK: You can set the table without a tablecloth.

[*She starts looking through some other boxes.*]

LEOLA: I always used a tablecloth — oh here it is - whenever I used these dishes. These dishes are meant to be set on a lovely tablecloth. Jimmy gave us this. Put that on. Such good taste.

[FRANK *opens the tablecloth and spreads it on the table as* LEOLA *looks over the dishware making sure she has everything she needs.*]

FRANK: We couldn't have done this last night? We couldn't have had a nice dinner on these dishes, on this tablecloth last night? You waited 'til now?

LEOLA: We could have. But we didn't. With getting everything else ready to go, making sure we we're all packed, I wasn't sure there would be time to do this. I'm better organized than I thought. [*She begins laying out the table.*] You here. My spot. Joanna. Gloria, Jimmy's spot. Just like the last time we were all together. Just the five of us. Before anybody got married or ... I was right to pick out these dishes. I knew standing there in the store, I'd live to regret it if I didn't"t get these dishes. Give us each a dessert plate and a salad plate. Is that salad plates you got there?

FRANK: What's it matter?

LEOLA: I want to take a picture of the dishes.

FRANK: You have pictures of the dishes.

LEOLA: Not like this.

FRANK: No. But pictures of the dishes at Thanksgiving and you had the table decorated with the wax Pilgrims for each of the kids. And at Christmas time.

LEOLA: So this will be the last of the series. All those other pictures with happy grinning holiday faces in them, and the turkey or the ham in the middle of the table. And this, this is how it ends. [*Pause.*] We need a moving van.

FRANK: One is on its way.

LEOLA: For a decoration. The theme of this table is moving. A moving van as a centerpiece and then for place cards, little boxes like packed cartons.

FRANK: Like these used to be.

LEOLA: You sit there. That's your spot and I'll take your picture. Then you take mine. Where's the camera? Get the camera.

FRANK: In the car.

LEOLA: In the car? What's it doing in the car?

FRANK: I want to take some pictures along the way.

LEOLA: Well, go get it.

FRANK: I still have to get some film.

LEOLA: So I'm not the only one who leaves something till the last minute, [*She looks at the table from different angles. She motions for him to join her.*] Doesn't that look nice?

FRANK: Yes. It looks very nice. [*Pause.*] Now put those dishes back in the boxes.

LEOLA: What's the rush?

FRANK: The movers …

LEOLA: The movers, the movers! If I can't take a picture for real, I'll take a picture of this with my eyes.

FRANK: And then will you pack them?

LEOLA: Sssh. I'm concentrating.

FRANK: You want a cup of coffee while you concentrate?

[LEOLA *puts up her hand to silence him. She stares at the dishes and then makes a "clicking" sound as if taking a picture.*]

LEOLA: What do you say I make us a nice breakfast? The table's all set. How about that?

FRANK: There's nothing in the refrigerator. We emptied it out.

LEOLA: Well, you run out and get something. How about ham and eggs? French toast? Yeah. Then you can pick up some film. I knew there was a reason we emptied out that refrigerator.

FRANK: Because we're moving. I thought we'd have some coffee. Maybe some toast ...

LEOLA: You have to do these things right. That's no kind of a last meal. Coffee and toast. Even convicts have better last meals.

FRANK: We're not walking the last mile. We're moving to Florida.

LEOLA: You have to leave a place right. It's too dark now. I was hoping to see the house one more time in the daylight.

FRANK: You've had weeks to see the house one more time.

LEOLA: Those times don't count. This is when it counts. You get in the car and look back at the house one more time. In the daylight. It'll be too sad leaving the house in the dark. This is the only house Jimmy ever knew. Or Gloria either. You don't leave a house alone in the dark that's been like that to people. I can't. I don't want to remember our house, have my last look at our house, being left all alone in the dark.

FRANK: It's a house Leola. I wanted to get a good hour or two in on the road before traffic picked up and then stop for some breakfast.

LEOLA: I'm not going.

FRANK: [*Pause.*] In the dark.

LEOLA: Or the daylight.

FRANK: The truck is on its way over.

LEOLA: I'm not moving.

FRANK: It'll be here soon.

LEOLA: I'm staying here.

FRANK: Everything else is packed. The house is sold. The Mitchells are moving in on Tuesday. The condominium is waiting for us in Miami.

LEOLA: We can unpack.

FRANK: They're painting the walls. That light green like you wanted, Celery color.

LEOLA: We'll get an apartment here. They have celery color paint here.

FRANK: I made a down payment.

LEOLA: They'll give it back. You changed your mind. You sell it. I'm too used to winter.

FRANK: You wanted summer year round.

LEOLA: So what's that? Dried out baked skin. I'll look like a prune in two weeks. We'll spend a fortune on skin creams. I've never used skin creams. Ever. I'm not starting now.

FRANK: Winter dries out your skin.

LEOLA: It's a different dry.

FRANK: Sun is healthy for you. We get some vitamin from it.

LEOLA: We get skin cancer from it.

FRANK: We were agreed. We discussed this for months. It was all settled.

LEOLA: I gave in.

FRANK: Then it's the first time.

LEOLA: I'm not going. I can't go. I won't know anybody. I won't have any friends.

FRANK: You make some. New ones.

LEOLA: I want the ones I have. The ones who gave us that farewell party. The ones who cried when they found out we were going to Miami. So far away. Almost not even in the country anymore.

FRANK: They'll visit us. They all have our address. The Russells ...

LEOLA: And you know how they'll have to get there? He doesn't see well enough to drive anymore. Fly.

FRANK: [*Slight pause.*] So they fly?

LEOLA: I am not having anyone anymore who I care about fly to see me. No more.

FRANK: Just because they fly doesn't mean ...

LEOLA: You can guarantee it? No. They drive to see me or they don't come.

FRANK: If people want to fly down to see us, we can't tell them they can't fly.

LEOLA: I can. I will. I mean that. I am not having anyone risk their life anymore to see me.

FRANK: Well, when the Russells come, driving, they'll be risking their lives. Especially with his eyes as bad as they are. And the Hudsons, driving. And the Harrisons, driving ...

LEOLA: Well, they may as well skip the visit. It won't be the same. It'll be like trying to talk to Moses.

FRANK: Moses? Moses who?

LEOLA: In the Bible Moses. Suppose you ran into Moses on the street. What would you have to talk to him about? What? He doesn't know about radio or TV or movies or ...

FRANK: But we know about movies and radio and TV.

LEOLA: You missed my point.

FRANK: I don't think there was a point.

LEOLA: There was a point. Never mind.

FRANK: There are all sorts of people for you to get to know.

LEOLA: I'm too old to start over with new people. All that introducing yourself, telling them where you were born, and where you've lived. And what you've done and what you wish you had done.

FRANK: They'll love to hear that. That's how it's done.

LEOLA: It's boring. I've had a dull life.

FRANK: You've had an interesting life.

LEOLA: They couldn't make a movie out of it.

FRANK: So? Who do you know whose life has been better?

LEOLA: I'm not talking about better or worse. I'm talking about sitting across a table from a bunch of people who don't know any of the places I know. They won't know the names of my friends. I'll have to fill them in on everything. That's so boring when you're telling a story, stopping every few seconds to get all the facts straight for a one minute episode about the time Rose O'Laughlin at work poured Coca Cola on the snake plant. I'll bore them.

FRANK: They all have Rose O'Laughlin stories.

LEOLA: I won't want to hear theirs. If I didn't know Rose and Margaret in the steno pool and Sally in bookkeeping I wouldn't want to hear about when Rose poured Coca Cola on the snake plant and it grew three inches in two days.

FRANK: I thought it was funny.

LEOLA: No you didn't.

FRANK: I laughed.

LEOLA: No. That was not laughing what you did. This is what you did. Just like this. [*She makes a coughing, hacking sound.*] You coughed.

FRANK: I laughed. I remember laughing.

LEOLA: It was a cough. It sounded like you were clearing your throat.

FRANK: That's how I laugh.

LEOLA: You don't laugh like that.

FRANK: I do too. At times. That's just how I do it.

LEOLA: When you feel obligated to laugh but you don't want to but think you should, you make a hacking sound. It may fool some people, but not me. I've been around you a long time.

FRANK: I have different laughs. For different stories. I laugh different ways. But that was a laugh.

LEOLA: When you think a story is funny, like the ones George Copinski tells, like those you laugh like this. [*She laughs loudly and rolls around on her chair.*] That's how you do it when you think something is funny.

FRANK: Yes. I laugh like that for some things. For off color jokes I laugh like that. But the Coca Cola story which was quite amusing and which will amuse a lot of other people — well, anyone with plants and there are a lot of those kinds of people in Miami like that — for that kind of a story you don't roll on the floor. It's a quieter sort of laugh. [*He coughs out a laugh.*]

LEOLA: That's just how you did it. Like you were taking your last breath. It sounded like you were choking and spitting up. I don't want to sit around with a bunch of strangers who sound like they're gagging when I tell them about myself.

FRANK: They won't. The Girardis are lovely people. Lovely. They had me in for coffee. They asked all about you.

LEOLA: We can move into an apartment around here. Westgate Village out by the highway! Very nice. Maureen Olson was there for a party and she just raved. And you know Maureen is not easily impressed.

FRANK: I'm not staying here. I went down to Miami, picked out a lovely condominium, three swimming pools, twelve laundry facilities, a supermarket two blocks away, I've written to Social Security already so they can send my checks to my new bank. We're moving. Drink your coffee.

LEOLA: You won't even drive by Westgate Village?

FRANK: It's not on the way to Miami.

LEOLA: Well then you have to promise me a few things.

FRANK: Like what?

LEOLA: Like I want you to … quit cigarettes. In that little, dinky condominium …

FRANK: It is not little. It is not dinky. You saw the floor plan.

LEOLA: With the windows sealed shut it'll smell awful the way you smoke around the clock.

FRANK: I've tried to give it up. You know what happens. I get those blisters on my lips.

LEOLA: I'm not going if you keep smoking. It's not fair to my lungs.

FRANK: Okay. I'll go to one of those clinics they have where they help you stop smoking. No, better yet, I'll get one of those patch things they're advertising all the time on the TV.

LEOLA: And since there will be a swimming pool handy …

FRANK: Not two hundred feet away. Very clean. I didn't even see any bugs in it.

LEOLA: I will want to swim.

FRANK: Good.

LEOLA: Which means I'll need to go to the hairdressers every day.

FRANK: For what?

LEOLA: My hair. I'm not wearing a cap in the pool. That doesn't save your hair anyway. It smashes the curl right out of it. I'll need to get it done every day. Maybe twice a day. Depending.

FRANK: On what?

LEOLA: If I go in twice a day. In the morning and maybe later in the afternoon.

FRANK: That's fifteen, twenty dollars a throw.

LEOLA: I can't do it myself. I can roll it up fine. But combing it out always defeats me. It'll look so bad it won't matter how good a job I did rolling it up. If we stayed here Margie Talbot could comb me out.

FRANK: Okay. You can get your hair done. If you go in that often I'm sure they can give you a better price.

LEOLA: I want new furniture.

FRANK: Ours is already to go with the movers. This furniture is free.

LEOLA: Not in a brand new condominium. With freshly painted walls. And with all new carpets. We'll need new.

FRANK: The truck is coming for this.

LEOLA: We can get rid of it down there. Maybe we can get a deal on it at the furniture place we go to.

FRANK: That green chair is only a year old.

LEOLA: Next to brand new it'll look fifteen or twenty. We're so well heeled. You're always saying so. So we'll get new furniture.

FRANK: Well heeled yes because I haven't been foolish with our money.

LEOLA: If you don't want to spend it on our apartment, I don't know what you will spend it on.

FRANK: Your hair.

LEOLA: That's only because I care how I look. Don't you want me to look nice? Don't you want that condominium to look nice? It costs money.

FRANK: Well maybe we should replace some of it.

LEOLA: All of it. I want to go Oriental.

FRANK: Oriental [*He thinks better of protesting further. Then, pleasantly.*] That will be very nice in that apartment with the celery green walls.

LEOLA: I want a maid. I want a cook. I'm sick of cleaning. I'm sick of cooking. And I want a chauffeur. Frankly anymore in the car with you I don't feel safe.

FRANK: Is that all?

LEOLA: Hair. Maid. Cook. Did I say cook?

FRANK: Yes.

LEOLA: I'm sick of cooking. Chauffeur.

FRANK: Furniture. Don't leave out furniture.

LEOLA: It'll look shabby. Cleaning lady. That's all.

FRANK: [*Pause.*] We're going to Miami. No cook. No maid. No chauffeur. I'm going to smoke. No new furniture.

LEOLA: Well then cancel the truck.

FRANK: Get dressed. Get your clothes on.

LEOLA: I don't want to go.

FRANK: Strip your bed. Put your sheets in the box.

LEOLA: I don't want to move.

FRANK: Get your clothes on and put your nightgown in your suitcase.

[LEOLA *starts looking through the boxes.*]

What are you looking for now?

[LEOLA *gets out a pot and finds a package of noodles.*]

What are you doing?

LEOLA: Making some noodles.

FRANK: Now?

LEOLA: I'm hungry for some buttered noodles. I'm upset, I get hungry.

FRANK: Have a piece of toast.

LEOLA: I am long past the point where a piece of toast will comfort me.

FRANK: You can't be cooking with the movers coming.

LEOLA: Why not? They're not taking the stove. What about that?

FRANK: What about what?

LEOLA: Maybe we should take the stove.

FRANK: We have a stove in the apartment. Now go strip your bed.

LEOLA: But not this stove. So many memories. I taught the kids how to cook on this stove. All of them. Gloria. And Joanna. And Jimmy. I think it's a mistake to leave this. You pack up, and leave all your memories behind.

FRANK: We'll make new memories.

LEOLA: What's wrong with the old ones?

FRANK: We'll add them to the new ones.

LEOLA: I stood right here with Jimmy, right on this spot, taught him how to make a tuna casserole ...

FRANK: Don't start on Jimmy now.

LEOLA: Who's starting? I'm remembering. What else do we have to do? Everything's packed.

FRANK: Almost everything.

[*She puts the pot back into the box and shuts the lid.*]

LEOLA: See how fast I can be packed? [*She returns to the stove.*] I stood right here. I think this is even the very spot. I think it is. I got the casserole I used in there someplace.

FRANK: Don't look for it now. This is not show and tell.

LEOLA: Visual aids come in handy. Like the stove. I stood right here.

FRANK: Maybe you want to take some of the floor.

LEOLA: I won't even dignify that. I stood right here. I told Jimmy how to grease the bowl, and then sprinkle it with bread crumbs to be the lining ...

FRANK: What the hell are you going on about Jimmy for now? You didn't even want to go to his memorial.

LEOLA: If we go to Florida, there won't be anything there of Jimmy. Nothing. He'll be all gone. Here he's still with us. Every place I look. He's still here.

FRANK: [*Carefully.*] No he isn't Leola.

LEOLA: I know he isn't. I'm not getting loony. But, it's only like he's out, gone out, someplace, not dead. I can think he's going to call me only he got too busy with stuff so maybe tomorrow, or over the weekend.

FRANK: He isn't going to call.

LEOLA: I know that.

FRANK: Sometimes I don't think you do. Really.

LEOLA: Do *you?*

FRANK: Every day.

LEOLA: So you're well adjusted.

FRANK: If you'd let yourself go at the memorial service. That's what they're for ...

LEOLA: Oh that memorial service. What was that?

FRANK: Well it was a lot more fitting than what you had in mind.

LEOLA: Fitting is as fitting does.

FRANK: Going to see some Barbra Streisand movie is no kind of fitting tribute.

LEOLA: Jimmy liked Barbra Streisand. He had all her records. And we went to see that first movie of hers, *Funny Girl*, and then later *Funny Lady*. And we saw *The Way We Were* on the TV once when he was visiting. So it would have been fitting.

FRANK: Well, you may as well have not been there. You hardly cried at all.

LEOLA: Yeah. I know. I was surprised too. I thought I would. That wasn't ever how I saw myself being when I used to think about it. Dry eyed.

FRANK: Think about it? You used to think about that?

LEOLA: I'd pretend to myself sometimes. I'd see people on TV being told some terrible thing, about someone they loved, and I'd think if anyone ever came here and told me that Jimmy was dead, how terrible that would be and I'd get so teary eyed just thinking about it, I'd go to pieces. Just thinking about it. And then I didn't when it did really happen. Maybe it got all used up when I was practicing.

FRANK: You'd pretend something like that?

LEOLA: Every now and then. If was watching something like that on the news. It's only normal.

FRANK: Normal? You call that normal? Crying when he isn't dead. And not crying when he is dead.

LEOLA: I'm sorry I wasn't a fountain of tears. But that's how I reacted.

FRANK: Well, I hope by the time I go -if I go first - your reactions are just a bit more in line with the rest of the world's. I don't want you sitting on your rear end in some movie theatre with me laid out some place and all our friends are wondering where in hell you are.

LEOLA: I wouldn't do that for you.

FRANK: Good. I can die in peace.

LEOLA: You don't like movies. There'd be no point.

FRANK: It was right that I took you to the church. That was the proper place I don't care what you say.

LEOLA: What's a church? I ask you that. What, when you think about it, what is a church?

FRANK: It's the place where his friends came from all over to organize a memorial tribute, a real one.

LEOLA: I wanted to do my own memorial my own way.

FRANK: Seeing some Barbra Streisand movie with your son not even five days dead was no kind of tribute anybody could understand.

LEOLA: Well that thing they staged wasn't so hot. What kind of memorial was that anyway? No body. No body to look at. Just some damn empty box that the funeral people would rent out again for another five hundred bucks. And don't think they don't. What kind of a memorial was that?

FRANK: The best they could do.

LEOLA: You were all so convinced he was dead.

FRANK: He was dead.

LEOLA: You got proof? He could be out there still. An amnesiac. And when you least expect it, boom, there he is knocking at the door, and we won't be here. We'll be in Florida. Only he won't know that.

FRANK: He isn't going to come knocking on the door. The plane blew up.

LEOLA: So they said.

FRANK: All the people blew up. 30,000 feet. He's dead. Don't you think?

LEOLA: He didn't need to die. If he'd stayed closer he wouldn't have been on that plane.

FRANK: You know why he lived far away.

LEOLA: [*With contempt.*] Yeah, yeah. His job. His life. His goals. His ambitions. So what?

FRANK: We wanted him to have ambitions.

LEOLA: I never should have sent him to those art classes when he was little. You were right, always pushing the sports at him. I should have let you have your way more, instead of all the time saying let him be interested in what he's interested in. I led him straight to his grave. I was a bad mother doing what I did. Those art classes lead to his death.

FRANK: No, no. You were a good mother. You know you were a good mother.

LEOLA: Yeah? Was I?

FRANK: He could have been a pro ball player and been on planes all the time.

LEOLA: Him? What kind of ball player could he have been? He was never on any teams.

FRANK: Okay, all right. A ... lawyer. A lawyer. He could have been a lawyer. Flying all over defending people, being on planes all the time.

LEOLA: A lawyer? Not with his gifts. He was gifted. They said so. In the 6th grade. "Your son is gifted." It wasn't just me who thought that.

FRANK: I'm only saying.

LEOLA: I know what you're saying. I killed him. Say it. You think it, say it. Don't hint. Say it. I killed him.

Frank: You didn't kill him. I'm only talking possibilities.

Leola: We must have done something he didn't like.

Frank: Nothing I know about. Nothing he ever said anything about.

Leola: Then why'd he leave us? Why didn't he stay here where people loved him?

Frank: He grew up.

Leola: Why'd he have to grow up? Why didn't he stay little? It was like he abducted himself; kidnapped himself away from us. Took himself away. Held himself hostage. I wasn't done yet. I wasn't through with him yet.

FRANK: I wasn't either.

LEOLA: I can shut my eyes — I don't even have to shut them — I can
see him clear, standing in his choir robe, the one he had when we were
going to the Methodist church, and I took his picture in it for our
Christmas card. And all the other times. I thought it was good having a memory. I hate my memory. You should not die before your
parents. You put your parents through so much anyway. At least they
should not have to be around when you die. There should be a law.

FRANK: A law?

LEOLA: A law of nature. A cosmic law. You should not see what you
brought into this world go out of it. It is not a nice thing. [*Crying.*]
Nothing. Nothing. We've got nothing.

[FRANK *goes to comfort her. She pulls away from him.*]

Not anything. Not one more look.

FRANK: Like you said. Over there. I see him getting the car keys. And
there, putting change left over from getting the milk and bread. And
there, watching TV. And there, standing at the refrigerator. I see him
a hundred times a day. [*He turns to her.*] You think he was only yours!
I got the news too! They told me too! We lost our boy. We did. Not
just you. We did.

[*She goes to him. She puts her hands on either side of his face.*]

LEOLA: Yes. Yes we did. We did.

[LEOLA *puts her arms around him. He then puts his arms around her. In
a moment she pulls away from him and returns to the table. She looks at
Jimmy's plate. She picks it up. She turns to* FRANK *and holds Jimmy's plate
out to him. He takes it and holds it. She picks up the carton for the dishes
and puts it on the table. She folds back the flaps and steps back.* FRANK *steps
forward and carefully puts Jimmy's plate in the box.* LEOLA *joins him and
they join hands, looking at the plate in the box. In a moment they separate
and begin silently packing the remaining dishes. In a bit, as they continue
to pack, they resume speaking.*]

You aren't afraid of how it'll be just you and me?

FRANK: Afraid of what?

LEOLA: Being alone.

FRANK: We've been alone before.

LEOLA: No. Never.

FRANK: Sure we have. Before the kids. After the kids.

LEOLA: Never. There's always been somebody to go to. Your parents. Mine. The kids. Your friends. My friends. Our friends. Now we're going to Miami where we won't know anybody. We'll be all alone. Together. In that apartment. Not even a backyard.

FRANK: We have a patio.

LEOLA: That's not what I mean. You missed my point.

FRANK: I did not. You're afraid we'll get there, we find out we don't have anything in common except for the years we spent together.

LEOLA: Aren't you? How often can we sit down and kick around 1959? Or Christmas 1967?

FRANK: We'll have new experiences.

LEOLA: Like finding out we don't have anything in common.

FRANK: We have a lot in common.

LEOLA: I needlepoint. You drink beer. I go to the library. You sleep on the couch.

FRANK: So I'll go to the library. I'll learn to sew. And you can sleep on the couch.

[*She makes a face. He takes the packed carton of dishes and sets it on the floor with the other cartons.*]

FRANK: [*Cont'd.*] You want us to have mutual activities. So do I. We have that in common. That's what got us here in the first place. I saw you at that dance in 1951 at the Aztec Ballroom on Montgomery. It was a Saturday. September the 15th. You had on a red dress.

LEOLA: My mother made it for me.

FRANK: You were lovely.

LEOLA: She made one in blue for my sister.

FRANK: It looked better in red. I said to David Morrison. I said, "See that girl? I want to have mutual activities in common with her." I wanted us to be alone together. But it's been like being at a dance being married to you. Someone always cutting in. But we always had the last dance together. Always. Didn't we?

LEOLA: Yes. You always told whoever barged in that the last dance was taken.

FRANK: I saw to it then and I'm seeing to it now. I want to be alone with you. If I didn't I'd have said, "Let's get an apartment around here. Let's stay close to friends. I don't want to be alone with you." But I didn't say that. Did I?

LEOLA: No. You said let's go to Miami.

FRANK: So I can finally have you all alone to myself. No more cutting in. I don't even want to share you with pots and pans.

LEOLA: You're going to wish I had a sinkfull of dishes. You're going to be so bored.

FRANK: I know how it's going to be. It's going to be like it was when we first met. We enjoyed that.

LEOLA: Yes. We did.

FRANK: I had to wait a long time back there in 1951 to get a dance with you. But it was worth it.

LEOLA: I remember when you put your hand on my back I thought, "Oh this is going to be a good dance. He knows how to lead." Some of those guys just couldn't. Larry Newman. He was lousy. I'd dance with him and it felt like I was dancing with a bulldozer. You knew how to lead though. I knew it the second we started.

[*She offers him her hand and they begin dancing. He is humming/singing.*]

Did I ever tell you the story about the time when Rose O'Laughlin poured Coca Cola on the snake plant on her desk and — honest to God, no lie — it grew 3 inches in 2 days.

[*He laughs uproaringly. She looks at him like he's nuts.*]

That story isn't that funny. You never laugh right.

[*They continue dancing and laughing as the lights fade.*]

THE END

Wendy Wasserstein

WAITING FOR PHILIP GLASS

Inspired By Shakespeare's Sonnet 94

Wendy Wasserstein

Wendy Wasserstein's play *The Heidi Chronicles* won the 1989 Pulitzer Prize, Tony Award, ad Susan Smith Blackburn Prize, the New York Drama Critics Circle, Drama Desk, and Outer Critic Awards; and earned her a grant from the Kennedy Center Fund for New American Plays. For *The Sisters Rosenweig* she received the 1993 Outer Critics Circle Award, a Tony Award nomination, and the William Inge Award for Distinguished Achievement in American Theatre. Other plays include *An American Daughter* (Lincoln Center); *Uncommon Women and Others* (Phoenix Theatre); *Isn't it Romantic* (Playwrights Horizon); a musical, *Miami* (with Jack Feldman and Bruce Sussman); and *Waiting for Philip Glass*, included in *Love's Fire* (The Acting Company). Her most recent play *Old Money* premiered at Lincoln Center in December 2000. Wasserstein's screenplays include *House of Husbands* (with Christopher Durang) and *The Object of My Affection*. For PBS Great Performances she has written *Kiss, Kiss Darling*; *Drive, She Said*; adaptations of John Cheever's *The Sorrows of Gin*, and her own *Uncommon Women and Others*. She adapted *The Heidi Chronicles* for TNT (1996 Emmy Award nomination for Best Television Movie) and *An American Daughter* for Lifetime Television. Her adaptation of The Nutcracker was performed at The American Ballet Theatre at The Met. Her books include essay collections *Shiksa Goddess* and *Bachelor Girls* (both Knopf) and *Pamela's First Musical*, a book for children (Hyperion). She has contributed to *The New Yorker*, *The New York Times*, and *Slate*, among many other publications. She has been the recipient of an NEA Grant, Guggenheim Fellowship, and most recently a Fellowship at the American Academy in Rome. She is a graduate of Mount Holyoke College and the Yale School of Drama.

Two women are standing in an East Hampton living room. The room is obviously the home of a contemporary collector. The women are around 35 and extremely attractive. SPENCER *wears a halter that shows off her well-sculptured body.* HOLDEN *wears a softer caftan, looking more ethereal.* SPENCER *is looking at a vase of lilies.*

HOLDEN: Do you think they're happy in there?

SPENCER: I've never seen your house look prettier. These flowers are amazing.

HOLDEN: Ecuadorian lilies. That doesn't mean they're happy in there.

SPENCER: Why wouldn't they be happy? They're eating. They're talking. And everybody's here.

HOLDEN: The guest of honor isn't here.

SPENCER: He'll be here. [*A couple walks by.* HARRY *and* LAURA *walk into the room.*]

HOLDEN: Hello, Harry! [*They wear matching sweaters over their shoulders.* HARRY *is excessively warm. He hugs both women.*]

HARRY: I'm so sorry we're late. We just came from Al's little thing for Henry Kissinger. What a great event! You know my wife, Laura Little? Laura, this is our gracious host. [*They shake hands.*]

HOLDEN: I admire your work. And this is Spencer Blumfeld.

SPENCER: [*Kisses* LAURA.] We know each other. You look so beautiful.

HOLDEN: Can I get you a drink? Philip Glass will be here any minute.

HARRY: Who's that?

SPENCER: The guest of honor. Tonight is a benefit for him.

LAURA: Harry, he's a very important avant-garde artist. Cutting edge. He directed *Einstein on the Beach*, which I, could sit through every night.

[HARRY *puts his arm around* LAURA.]

HARRY: We popped over to Spain last week for the Guggenheim opening in Bilbao. I can't tell you how exciting that little museum is. [*He kisses her.*]

LAURA: I'm training Harry to start thinking globally. It's our job to keep up.

[*He kisses her again.*]

HARRY: Everyone thinks I married her for her looks. It's not true, I did it for her energy.

LAURA: Honey, I think I'd like some water.

HARRY: No ice. Lime.

[*They walk into the next room.*]

HOLDEN: Robert Wilson.

SPENCER: What?

HOLDEN: She thinks she's here to see Robert Wilson. He directed *Einstein on the Beach*. Our guest is the composer.

SPENCER: She won't know the difference.

HOLDEN: Do you think she's a good writer?

SPENCER: If you think an overrated sex column is good writing.

HOLDEN: Harry's a very nice man but ...

SPENCER: But you could never marry him. Not even just for five years to fulfill the prenup? 'Cause she'll be leaving him the day after. That's not a diamond on her finger. It's a satellite dish.

HOLDEN: I'd do anything for this night to be over.

SPENCER: You can't be cuckoo enough to think they were madly in love.

HOLDEN: Why not? It would have been nice.

SPENCER: But highly unlikely.

HOLDEN: I'm just not up for this. I look enormous and ancient.

SPENCER: I think you look great. But if you're unhappy, I'm thrilled with my eyelift.

HOLDEN: You look fabulous.

SPENCER: Our health and beauty department has done the research. When a woman turns 35 it's blastoff for corrective surgery. Any later you lose the skin's elasticity. I'm giving you great advice and you're not listening to me.

HOLDEN: I just wish he would goddamn get here.

SPENCER: Who? Have you invited someone else I should know about?

HOLDEN: No. The guest of honor. The artist in question. And I wish everyone hadn't just seen each other at Alan's perfect little thing for Henry Kissinger. And furthermore, where the fuck is Diane Sawyer?

SPENCER: Take it easy. I thought you said that shrink of yours is helping you.

HOLDEN: She's helping me with the memory of my mother who lowered my self-esteem by competing with me for attention from my withholding father. That has nothing to do at all with this evening being done and over.

SPENCER: I give up. I really don't know what you want.

HOLDEN: I want Diane Sawyer here. And I want Philip Glass here. [*A balding man of around 35 comes into the room. He is not conventionally attractive but commands attention. He is compulsively eating crudités.*]

GERRY: You changed caterers. I hate caviar in baby bliss potatoes. Give me a cocktail frank or Swedish meatball any day. How are you, Spencer?

SPENCER: I'm terrific, Gerry. Congratulations on your marriage. I met your wife's dad in Washington the other day.

GERRY: Are you spending a lot of time with the Secretary of Transportation?

SPENCER: It was a party at Ben Bradlee's and Sally Quinn's for our September issue.

GERRY: Well you certainly caused a nice little buzz with that.

SPENCER: Thank you. I didn't know you read women's magazines.

GERRY: I read everything. But you should do more about emerging Hollywood. No one cares about Michelle Pfeiffer and her babies anymore.

SPENCER: Holden, can I get you another spritzer?

HOLDEN: I'm fine. Thanks.

GERRY: Honey, she just wants an excuse to run and tell everyone she can't believe what I just said to her.

SPENCER: I'll bring you back a Swedish meatball. [*SPENCER leaves the room.*]

GERRY: I've never understood your interest in that woman. She's a hideous climber and everyone says she's going to be fired. That September issue was a total embarrassment. And the entire company's up for sale anyway.

HOLDEN: Are you buying it?

GERRY: Boring. It's no fun if it's just about making money. I'd rather stay home with my wife. You're looking well.

HOLDEN: Thank you.

GERRY: Kids are good?

HOLDEN: Kids are great. Kip's in Maine and Taylor's at this terrific summer camp in Cambodia. She's learning to plant rice and dig her own latrine.

GERRY: So you won't have to tip the doorman at 873 Park Avenue to do it anymore.

HOLDEN: That was an easy shot.

GERRY: You set it up.

HOLDEN: I read you bought that English publishing house.

GERRY: Now this is seriously interesting. You buy the world's largest chain of discount drugstores and nobody notices. You buy Jonathan Swift's bankrupt publishing house and Henry Kissinger's congratulating you. By the way, you should have come to Alan's little thing for him.

HOLDEN: Well I was here. Organizing my own little thing.

GERRY: I'd say it was the classiest event of the summer. The regulars like Mike and Diane Sawyer were there but there were some neat surprises, too.

HOLDEN: Diane Sawyer was there?

GERRY: And Bill Bradley, Steven Spielberg, April Gornick, and Erik Fischl.

HOLDEN: The painters?

GERRY: Alan is considered a major collector now. Rina and I ran into him at the Guggenheim opening in Bilbao. You have got to get there. You know I never thought much of Gehry's work but he has really hit his stride. But if I had to do it all over again I'd be an architect.

HOLDEN: Then you'd have to listen to other people's opinions.

GERRY: I'd hate that.

HOLDEN: I know.

GERRY: A lot of your friends were there and Harry and the sexpert. She should be sued for malpractice for those columns. I've tried those positions and they're only possible for a spastic giraffe or a lesbian hydra.

HOLDEN: Gerry, shh. They're here.

GERRY: Why do you let these kinds of people into your house?

HOLDEN: He's a friend of mine.

GERRY: She's an ex-lover of mine. That doesn't mean I have to feed her. I have to say I was very lucky. After my first marriage there was basically you and Rina. You two were the standouts.

HOLDEN: Well, at least we had the most quotable fathers. So you liked Bilbao?

GERRY: You really don't want to talk about us. Or why until tonight you've avoided meeting my new wife.

HOLDEN: I'm just waiting for Philip Glass.

GERRY: Why don't you tell your guests if they write a check they can all go home now. All they want is to be excused. We all just saw each other with Henry Kissinger anyhow.

HOLDEN: You don't have to stay, Gerry ...

GERRY: I have to stay, I'm only here for you. [*Kisses her.*] Where's that guy you've been dating?

HOLDEN: He's inside.

GERRY: I heard he's a something.

HOLDEN: Developer.

GERRY: Sounds promising. What does he develop?

HOLDEN: Pennsylvania.

GERRY: You can do better.

HOLDEN: What's the matter with Pennsylvania?

GERRY: Nothing. Except Liberty Bell condos.

HOLDEN: How do you know the name of his condos?

GERRY: I pay attention. That's my business. Holden, you don't need to throw it all away on some dolt who drives a Lexus. Does he wear Gucci loafers? 'Cause it would kill me to see you with a guy in Gucci loafers. At least wait till you're 40.

HOLDEN: He wears Hermès loafers.

GERRY: Are you doing this deliberately?

[RINA, *a beautiful young woman of around 22 comes into the room. She is dressed in something resembling a slip.*]

There you are. We were just talking about you. [*He kisses her.*]

RINA: This is such a beautiful house.

GERRY: I think it's one of Bobby Stern's better ones. Delightful play of air and light. Holden's father had it built.

HOLDEN: It was kind of a first wedding present.

GERRY: Holden's father was a philosophy professor at Princeton. Wonderful man. Sort of my idol.

HOLDEN: He was alcoholic and married five times before his suicide.

GERRY: But he spent his life paying attention to what truly interested him. Of course I have no robber barons in my family so that was never an option for me.

RINA: These are beautiful lilies. Where are they from?

HOLDEN: Ecuador. They're much heartier than the ones from Holland.

GERRY: Holden does her own flowers.

HOLDEN: It's a hobby of mine. My daughter asked me once why I hired a man to put flowers into a vase.

[*They all laugh uncomfortably. A burly man in a Gucci belt and loafers comes into the room.*]

JOE: So where's the guest of honor?

HOLDEN: He's on his way. Joe, I don't think you know my friend Gerry Gavshon.

JOE: No, but of course I'm always reading about you. Congratulations on that Binmart deal. You're killing every discount store in my part of the country.

GERRY: We're opening next month in Moscow and Beijing. Who knew that in our lifetime we could say we made the world safe for Alka-Seltzer. This is my wife, Rina. Are yon a big fan of Philip Glass?

JOE: Holden took me to see something of his.

HOLDEN: *Glass Pieces*. The Jerome Robbins ballet.

JOE: The one with those gorgeous young people going across the stage.

GERRY: That could be a lot of things.

HOLDEN: No, Joe, you're right. I know the one you mean.

JOE: Personally, I like a song that goes somewhere. But you've got to give them both credit. It was a lively show and most of the time ballet except for the jumpers can be really boring.

HOLDEN: Do yon go to the ballet, Rina?

GERRY: We prefer the opera. We're going practically every free evening. I used to be intimidated but it's really very easy to pick up.

JOE: That's the way to stay young. Learn something new. Have you ever been on an Outward Bound trip?

GERRY: Spending the night alone on a mountain in Colorado? I'm from the suburbs of Pittsburgh, Joe. I know the answer. I'd never survive without takeout Chinese.

JOE: You eat a few roots and you're fine. Listen, I've been with them on Hurricane Island, I've sailed a Viking ship down a fjord, but last week I did something extraordinary. I went solo to the South Bronx for a night. Terrible neighborhood. Crack vials on the street. People you think if you look them in the face you'll never see your kids again. And I made it through. First time I've been really scared in years.

RINA: Once the baby's born I want to teach cooking at a Phoenix House in the South Bronx.

GERRY: Sweetie, they don't need to learn fat-free cooking at a Phoenix House in the South Bronx.

HOLDEN: When is your baby due?

RINA: Next March. Gerry wants a large family. I told him now that we've got the ranch even six kids is okay with me.

HOLDEN: What ranch?

GERRY: We got a little place in Jackson Hole. Around one thousand acres. And it's easy to get to if you don't rely on commercial airlines. We just pop over to Teterboro and we're there. Believe me it makes a lot more sense than driving to the Berkshires.

[SPENCER *comes back into the room.*]

SPENCER: Honey, people are beginning to start leaving. Nora told me to give you a big kiss but she had to meet Diane Sawyer, and Kathleen Turner says she had to rush out before her babysitter turned psycho.

[HARRY *and* LAURA *come out.*]

HARRY: We heard he wasn't coming.

HOLDEN: He's on his way.

HARRY: Honey, we're expected for dinner.

GERRY: Whose dinner?

HARRY: Just Joe and Patty. Are you going?

GERRY: He's a second-rate talent. With a gift for schmoozing. And she's lucky she hasn't been indicted.

LAURA: I thought they were friends of yours.

HARRY: You two know each other?

GERRY: We're acquainted. Nice seeing you again.

LAURA: Nice seeing you again. It was a great party, Holden. Please tell Mr. Glass I'm one of his greatest fans.

GERRY: Laura …

LAURA: Yes.

GERRY: I really enjoyed your last column.

LAURA: Thank you. Good night.

…..[*They exit.*]

JOE: What does she write about?

GERRY: Blow jobs.

JOE: That takes guts.

SPENCER: She can't help herself.

HOLDEN: I better go in there and tell them he's on his way.

JOE: Maybe we should invite everyone out for dinner. Nothing wrong with having lobster and white wine overlooking the ocean.

SPENCER: And we could all reenact *Einstein on the Beach.*

HOLDEN: You go ahead.

JOE: What?

HOLDEN: You go ahead. I can't leave my guests.

JOE: I wouldn't leave you at your party.

HOLDEN: No, please, take Spencer and get a lobster on the beach.

SPENCER: What are you talking about?

HOLDEN: I prefer that you go.

SPENCER: Gerry, this is your fault.

GERRY: I didn't say a word.

SPENCER: Why did you come here?

GERRY: I was invited. I wanted my old friend to meet my wife.

HOLDEN: Rina and Gerry bought a ranch where they're hoping to raise a family.

GERRY: You're not giving Rina the credit she's due. Rina graduated Phi Beta Kappa from Bowdoin. She got into Harvard Medical School.

RINA: Gerry, you don't have to tell everyone that.

GERRY: Why not? It happens to be true. And Rina's setting up the Rina and Gerry Gavshon Pediatrics Foundation.

RINA: I think I would like to go home now. I'm feeling a little tired.

GERRY: We can't leave now.

RINA: Would you drop me at home?

JOE: Of course.

GERRY: What are you doing?

RINA: My feet are hurting. I need to lie down.

GERRY: You can lie down here until the guess of honor comes.

JOE: Spencer and I will take you home.

HOLDEN: You're a gentleman, Joe.

JOE: I'll just drop her off and be right back.

HOLDEN: You don't have to.

SPENCER: Are you insane?

HOLDEN: No. I'm waiting for Philip Glass. [*She kisses* SPENCER *on the cheek.*] Good night.

GERRY: You just sent a perfectly nice man away.

HOLDEN: I thought I shouldn't throw myself away on a dolt who drives a Lexus.

GERRY: Yon shouldn't listen so carefully to everything I say.

HOLDEN: Your wife is charming. I liked her a lot.

GERRY: She gets tired. But when you total it all up she makes the most sense.

HOLDEN: A good long-term investment.

GERRY: Don't be crude.

HOLDEN: I didn't get to Bilbao. I am crude. Would yon excuse me while I retrieve my party?

[*He grabs her by the arm.*]

GERRY: What the hell is wrong with you?

HOLDEN: Nothing. I just want to tell them to wait. That's all.

GERRY: It makes no difference if they wait.

HOLDEN: But our guest will come and tell us all what it's like to be an artist. What it's like to think you can make up a life that's different from your own.

GERRY: There's nothing wrong with your life.

HOLDEN: You're absolutely right there's nothing wrong with it at all.

GERRY: Let me take you to dinner tonight? After he leaves.

HOLDEN: I can't. I have a date.

GERRY: Your date just left.

HOLDEN: He's not my only date.

GERRY: So you're leaving me here alone.

HOLDEN: Good for me. Bad for you. Isn't that what you once told me in business had to be true.

GERRY: This isn't business. This is friendship.

HOLDEN: I'm tired of friendship. Good night, Gerry. [*She kisses* GERRY.] Thank you so much for dropping by.

GERRY: You have no idea how much I respect you.

HOLDEN: It's great news about Binmart in Moscow!

GERRY: [*Suddenly yells.*] Talk to me, Holden! [*She takes the lilies out of the vase.*]

HOLDEN: These are for Rina.

GERRY: Please, you don't have to.

HOLDEN: Most likely I won't be here in the morning. And lilies that fester smell far worse than weeds. Good night. [*She watches as* GERRY *leaves the room.* HOLDEN *stands up, pulls herself up straight, and walks into the adjoining room.*] Everyone. He's on his way.

END

SONNET 94

They that have pow'r to hurt and will do none,
That do not do the thing they most do show,
Who, moving others, are themselves as stone,
Unmoved, cold, and to temptation slow—
They rightly do inherit heaven's graces,
And husband Nature's riches from expense;
They are the lords and owners of their faces,
Others but stewards of their excellence.
The summer's flow'r is to the summer sweet,
Though to itself it only live and die;
But if that flow'r with base infection meet,
The basest weed outbraves his dignity:
For sweetest things turn sourest by their deeds;
Lilies that fester smell far worse than weeds.

BEST AMERICAN SHORT PLAYS
1998-1999

The Likeness by THEODORE APSTEIN • Home by LAURA CAHILL • Fifteen Minutes by DAVE DECHRISTOPHER • No Crime by BILLY GODA • I Dream Before I Take The Stand by ARLENE HUTTON • Reverse Transcription by TONY KUSHNER • Jade Mountain by DAVID MAMET • What Drove Me Back to Reconsidering My Father by JOHN FORD NOONAN • Deux-X by JULES TASCA • Boundary County, Idaho by TOM TOPOR • All About Al by CHERIE VOGELSTEIN

$15.95 • PAPER • ISBN: 1-55783-429-6 • $32.95 • CLOTH• ISBN: 1-55783-425-3

BEST AMERICAN SHORT PLAYS
1997-1998

Belly Fruit by MARIA BERNHARD, SUSSANAH BLINKOFF, JANET BORRUS • Little Airplanes of the Heart by STEVE FEFFER • The Most Massive Woman Wins by MADELEINE GEORGE • The White Guy by STEPHEN HUNT • Time Flies by DAVID IVES • The Confession of Many Strangers by LAVONNE MUELLER • OEDI by RICH ORLOFF • Creative Development by JACQUELYN REINGOLD • The Man Who Couldn't Stop Crying by MURRAY SCHISGAL • The Trio by SHEL SILVERSTEIN

$15.95 • PAPER • ISBN 1-55783-426-1 • $32.95 • CLOTH • ISBN 1-55783-365-6

BEST AMERICAN SHORT PLAYS
1996-1997

Misreadings by NEENA BEEBER • The Rehearsal: A Fantasy by J. RUFUS CALEB • The Vacuum Cleaner by EDWARD de GRAZIA • Mrs. Sorken by CHRISTOPHER DURANG • Four Walls by GUS EDWARDS • I'm With Ya, Duke by HERB GARDNER • My Medea by SUSAN HANSELL • I Didn't Know You Could Cook by RICH ORLOFF • Tunnel of Love by JACQUELYN REINGOLD • Fifty Years Ago by MURRAY SCHISGAL • Your Everyday Ghost Story by LANFORD WILSON • Wildwood Park by DOUG WRIGHT

$15.95 • PAPER • ISBN 1-55783-317-6 • $29.95 • CLOTH • ISBN 1-55783-316-8

BEST AMERICAN SHORT PLAYS 1993-1994

"THE WORK IS FIRST RATE! IT IS EXCITING TO FIND THIS COLLECTION OF TRULY SHORT PLAYS BY TRULY ACCOMPLISHED PLAYWRIGHTS...IDEAL FOR SCHOOL READING AND WORKSHOP PRODUCTIONS:...' —KLIATT

Window of Opportunity by JOHN AUGUSTINE • Barry, Betty, and Bill by RENÉE TAYLOR/JOSEPH BOLOGNA • Come Down Burning by KIA CORTHRON • For Whom the Southern Belle Tolls by CHRISTOPHER DURANG • The Universal Language by DAVID IVES • The Midlife Crisis of Dionysus by GARRISON KEILLOR • The Magenta Shift by CAROL K. MACK • My Left Breast by SUSAN MILLER • The Interview by JOYCE CAROL OATES • Tall Tales from The Kentucky Cycle by ROBERT SCHENKKAN • Blue Stars by STUART SPENCER • An Act of Devotion by DEBORAH TANNEN • Zipless by ERNEST THOMPSON • Date With A Stranger by CHERIE VOGELSTEIN

$15.95 • PAPER • ISBN: 1-55783-199-8 • $29.95 • CLOTH• ISBN: 1-55783-200-5

BEST AMERICAN SHORT PLAYS 1992-1993

Little Red Riding Hood by BILLY ARONSON • Dreamers by SHEL SILVERSTEIN • Jolly by DAVID MAMET • Show by VICTOR BUMBALO • A Couple With a Cat by TONY CONNOR • Bondage by DAVID HENRY HWANG • The Drowning of Manhattan by JOHN FORD NOONAN • The Tack Room by RALPH ARZOOMIAN • The Cowboy, the Indian, and the Fervent Feminist by MURRAY SCHISGAL • The Sausage Eaters by STEPHEN STAROSTA • Night Baseball by GABRIEL TISSIAN • It's Our Town, Too by SUSAN MILLER • Watermelon Rinds by REGINA TAYLOR • Pitching to the Star by DONALD MARGULIES • The Valentine Fairy by ERNEST THOMPSON • Aryan Birth by ELIZABETH PAGE

$15.95 • Paper • ISBN 1-55783-166-1 • $29.95 • cloth • ISBN 1-55783-167-X

BEST AMERICAN SHORT PLAYS
1991-1992
Edited by Howard Stein and Glenn Young

The Best American Short Play series includes a careful mixture of offerings from many prominent established playwrights, as well as up and coming younger playwrights. This collection of short plays truly celebrates the economy and style of the short play form. Doubtless, a must for any library!

Making Contact by **PATRICIA BOSWORTH** • Dreams of Home by **MIGDALIA CRUZ** • A Way with Words by **FRANK D. GILROY** • Prelude and Liebestod by **TERRENCE MCNALLY** • Success by **ARTHUR KOPIT** • The Devil and Billy Markham by **SHEL SILVERSTEIN** • The Last Yankee by **ARTHUR MILLER** • Snails by **SUZAN-LORI PARKS** • Extensions by **MURRAY SCHISGAL** • Tone Clusters by **JOYCE CAROL OATES** • You Can't Trust the Male by **RANDY NOOJIN** • Struck Dumb by **JEAN-CLAUDE VAN ITALLIE** and **JOSEPH CHAIKIN** • The Open Meeting by **A.R.GURNEY**

$12.95 • PAPER • ISBN: 1-55783-113-0 $25.95 • CLOTH• ISBN: 1-55783-112-2

BEST AMERICAN SHORT PLAYS 1990

Salaam, Huey Newton, Salaam by **ED BULLINS** • Naomi in the Living Room by **CHRISTOPHER DURANG** • The Man Who Climbed the Pecan Trees by **HORTON FOOTE** • Teeth by **TINA HOWE** • Sure Ting by **DAVID IVES** • Christmas Eve on Orchard Street by **ALLAN KNEE** • Akhmatova by **ROMULUS LINNEY** • Unprogrammed by **CAROL MACK** • The Cherry Orchard by **RICHARD NELSON** • Hidden in this Picture by **AARON SORKIN** • Boy Meets Girl by **WENDY WASSERSTEIN** • Abstinence by **LANFORD WILSON**

$24.95 CLOTH ISBN 1-55783-084-3 • $12.95 PAPER ISBN 1-55783-085-1

APPLAUSE